Are You Free?

The Heart of God is Easy to Please,
Hard to Satisfy

Bjorn Stavness

ABUNDANT HARVEST
PUBLISHING

Are You Free?
Copyright © 2019 by Bjorn Stavness
Revised 2023

ALL RIGHTS RESERVED
No portion of this book may be reproduced, stored in any retrieval system, or transmitted in any form or by any means, electronic, mechanical, photocopy, recording or otherwise, without the express written consent of the author.

Editing/Formatting: Erik V. Sahakian
Cover Design/Layout: Andrew Enos

All Scripture is taken from the New King James Version of the Bible. Copyright © 1979, 1980, 1982 by Thomas Nelson, Inc. Used by permission. All rights reserved.

Library of Congress Control Number: 2018965516

ISBN 978-1-7327173-0-5
First Printing: March 2019

FOR INFORMATION CONTACT:

Abundant Harvest Publishing
www.abundantharvestpublishing.com

Printed in the United States of America

Books written by Bjorn Stavness

Are You Free?

Are You Living?

Are You Lovable?

Are You Listening?

Are You Convinced?

This book contains hard fought after truths. For over 25 years I have ministered God's truths to free people from every imaginable stronghold. Not once a week in a counseling setting, but living alongside broken people for months, sometimes years, forced me to turn my Biblical platitudes into life-changing truths.

Thank you, to the over 5,000 people that chose to search for God's wisdom in your time of utter hopelessness at the House of Decision, a woman's home, and the House of Opportunity, a men's home. What is written on these pages constitutes the liberating principles that God taught me as I shared His truths with you.

www.houseofdecision.com

CONTENTS

Opening Thoughts…………………………..……....7

Part One:
Reversing Shame

1. Return to Sender……………………………………14
2. Humble Down……………………………………25
3. Party Killer…………………………………..…28
4. Wallowing In Shame……..……………………..…33

Part Two:
Freedom In Christ

5. Selfishness Strangles Freedom …………………….41
6. Recognize Your Enemy ……..….…............……..53
7. Love Decides ……………………..……………..61
8. God's Trash Talk ………………….....……..74
9. Flavor Freedom.. ……..………………...….……82
10. Following Instructions ……………………...….…89
11. Walking Out What God Has Worked In……...…..... 99
12. Are You Free? ……………………..………...108

13. Unfair …… …………………………………..….118

Part Three:
Freedom Truths

14. Flavor Freedom ……..………......…………………..128
15. Easy to Please, Hard to Satisfy …………………139
16. Where the Love War is Fought ………………….151
17. All For Oneness …………..........................………155
18. True Repentance …………………………………..160
19. Choosing a Father ………...……………………….164
20. The Rhino and the Flea …………………….…......175
21. SIN's Painful Enslavements …………………….…189
22. No Belief Bias….. ……………………….....................195
23. Hell's Appetizers………. ……………….................200
24. Seeing Hell With God's Eyes…………….…........204
25. Forgiveness With A Gift…………………...…...208
26. Bypassing Words…………………………….….......224

Final Thoughts ……………………………….…......230
About the Author………………………………...….231

All biblical truths point to oneness, first with God, then with each other.

Christ's cross embraces God's cure for the twoness that sin caused and restores the oneness that brings us freedom to live one with Him in our lives.

Dust and Deity made one.

Nothing this world offers competes with the quality of oneness we walk in with God and then share with each other.

You before me, but Jesus before you.

"I in them, and You in Me; that they may be made perfect in one, and that the world may know that You have sent Me, and have loved them as You have loved Me."

John 17:23

Opening Thoughts

Imagine an eight-year-old is asked, "What would you do if you knew for certain that there would never be any consequences? No consequences for your actions—not now or ever. Not even in heaven."

What comes to the child's mind? Perhaps something like *If I never got in trouble, I would take all the best toys from the store and play with them. And eat all the candy too. And I'd smack that bully, Billy, right in his big mouth!*

It'd be something along those lines, right?

Now imagine *you* are asked the same question. There would be absolutely no consequences. None, never. What actions come to your mind? Instead of responding quickly, stop reading and let your mind wander. What would you do?

....

Did you also think of something you could get away with? *If I never got in trouble, I would...* Maybe an attractive movie star to be with? A beautiful car or beach house to take? A vacation spot to call your own? Someone to get even with?

Or, when you thought of "no consequences" for your actions, did something like *I would secretly help someone who could not pay me back* go through your head?

Notice what direction your mind gravitates toward when the only criterion given is "no consequences." Why? Does that not glaringly reveal to us something spot-on about our nature if left to serve itself without consequences?

Here is a short summary of the basic mechanics of our spiritual birth nature.

The correct two choices to choose between for our birth nature are, "Are we born selfless or selfish?" Not, "Are we born good or evil."

We are born innocent, yet selfish. Innocent because we did nothing to deserve our self-driven bent. Our hearts only "want to" is ultimately to please ourselves. All our goodness has a return address attached, even if only for personal praise or pacifying guilt.

We didn't cause our birth nature problem, nor does God require us to fix it. Jesus Christ did that for us on His cross. He paid the price to release us from the iron grip of selfishness and freed us to live selflessly by imparting His pure character within us. And, along with implanting His new nature within us, He forgives us of all the offenses created by our selfish nature (First Peter 1:3; First John 1:9).

What God does require of us is to accept the gift of His nature by welcoming His Spirit to manage our lives and by humbly accepting His payment for our offenses. We must humbly recognize that we have a "need beyond our ability." What is our basic need? We don't possess the power to change our "want to" from selfish to selfless.

Anyone can change their outward behavior from evil actions to good actions without God, but no one can change their disposition any more than a zebra can change its stripes. Without God, folks might upgrade their lives from self-destructive to helping others, but underneath, for the actions themselves, the only motive available remains self-serving.

Again, if we want to overcome our selfish birth nature and then experience oneness with Him, He must first implant His selfless nature within us. Then we are no longer divided from Him, but living as one. Only then can we produce acts of goodness that possess a quality of love that are truly compatible with God's nature. Supernaturally and beyond our comprehension, God directs our spirit by His Spirit. Both reside in our bodies made from dust. Dust and Deity are united as one, walking life's journey together (John 17:23).

Does this sound far-fetched? Can God really invade our hearts and minds? Does He genuinely desire to be close to us as we walk our life's journey?

That God takes pleasure in closeness with us should not surprise us. Thinking that God sits disengaged on a distant planet makes no sense when examining our own makeup. When God created man, He created him in His own image.

"Let *Us* make man in *Our* image" (Genesis 1:26).

Not "Me in My image," but "Us in Our image." What is God's image? He is one God in three Persons, enjoying perfect harmony. The Tri-unity. Oneness. God fashioned humankind, like Himself, to delight in oneness. First with Him and then with each other.

Oneness embraces our most fulfilling purpose in life and only God knows how best to perfect it. His Word teaches us and His indwelling Spirit guides us.

Is it any wonder why the things that matter most, that cause us the greatest joy or pain, relate to oneness shared or oneness broken? Above all else we want to love and be loved. We crave intimacy because God imparted that craving to us from Himself. We definitely didn't inherit our desire for oneness from a sea sponge!

Our built-in deep desire to share our lives with others comes from God. And naturally, He wants the same thing— to love and be loved back.

God intensely desires to share His life with us and He truly enjoys our sharing our lives with Him. "I have called you friends" (John 15:15).

Part One

Reversing Shame

First, the difference between guilt and shame:

Guilt:

We feel guilty after our conscience tells us we did something wrong. Maybe we deceived our spouse or friend. Or stole from our co-worker. Or committed adultery. We know we painfully hurt someone and need their forgiveness to restore our relationship.

Our guilt is relieved if the injured person forgives us. They "buried the hatchet." Or, let go of a grudge. We feel comforted that the relationship is on the path to being restored. After being forgiven, we enjoy a sense of freedom, thankful that the person we hurt wants to reconcile and remove any animosity that we created between us and them.

Shame:

Shame, however, travels deeper into our soul. Shame attacks how we see ourselves, making it far harder than guilt to wash off. Even after we receive forgiveness, we still know something remains badly broken at our core. "What kind of pitiful person steals from their kind-hearted co-worker?" Or, "I apologized for lying but I still feel like a pathetic scumbag for lying in the first place." Shame relates to the contemptable way we see ourselves in the mirror.

"I know that my spouse forgives me of my adultery, *but that only speaks highly of them*. I am looking at a slim-ball bottom-feeder when I look at myself in our wedding photos."

....

Both guilt and shame make us feel miserable. With God, our guilt is removed by the forgiveness Jesus offers by His cross, speaking highly of His gracious love for us to reconcile. Shame, though, reflects what we still know about our miserable self, "I am forgiven and going to heaven because Jesus forgave me and He keeps His word. But, knowing my disgusting past, some angel will probably sneak me in heaven's back door that God uses for the sleaze-balls that accepted Jesus' forgiveness."

Seems like shame requires stronger detergent.

Knowing the difference between guilt and shame, and realizing how deep shame buries its claws into our soul, have you ever questioned, "Hmmm, did Christ die to remove my shame as well as my guilt?"

Maybe you wondered, "How on God's green earth can my haunting shame coexist with the abundant joy that Jesus promised?"

Or perhaps hoped, "When Satan tries to rub my nose in my disgusting past, did Jesus make a way for me to turn it around and make him regret his attempt to shame me?"

Those questions will soon be answered.

1
Return to Sender

Do we have the spiritual power to go on the offensive and rub Satan's nose in our prior obedience to him, throwing our shame back on Him? If so, how do we get our shame off of ourselves and send it back to Satan?

To place our shame on Satan, we start by understanding how Jesus willingly chose to carry shame His entire life, all the way to His cross.

The road Christ purposely walked, decided before time, didn't start with being born into royalty, demanding the respect of the Jews from His kingly palace. Even though Jesus came to die for the world's sins, He didn't dress in elegant clothes, stand on the temple steps, and proudly proclaim, "I am the noble Savior of the world. I will willfully sacrifice My innocent life for this pitiful world as you all sing My praises and bow down to worship Me." Then, greatly honored by all, fall on His own sword. 1 Peter 1:20, Phil. 2:5-11, Revelations 13:8

Instead, Jesus was mocked for being born out of wedlock, in a smelly barn, in a humble town. His first thirty years were spent in obscurity as a commoner.

At His trial and crucifixion, Jesus was "reviled" and "insulted" by the same people He fed and healed. Their verbal and physical abuse went far deeper than "This is Your sentence for Your crime." *The crowds condemned Jesus as a vile person who should feel disgusted with His own behavior.*

To "revile" means they turned against Him with contempt, someone deserving to be spit on and humiliated. To mock His Person, they pulled out His beard, put a purple robe on Him and made a special thorny crown to force onto His head.

"He is a disgrace. A complete fraud. A con man of the worst sort. He preached kindness and healed the sick to convince us He cares for us, but He lied the entire time about the imposter He really was. His bloody swollen face and shredded back are proof He knew He was two-faced from the beginning." Isaiah 53:1-10, Psalms 38:12-14, Matthew 27:39-44, Mark 15:29-32, Luke 22:64,56, 23:34-39

Not miraculously saving Himself from the cruelty of the Romans reinforced their accusations. To the Jews, His humiliating death was His well-deserved punishment for His deceitful claims. "He willfully betrayed and ruined people's lives that believed His teachings, a far greater spiritual offense that outweighs all the physical goodness He did. We will eagerly set a murderer free if it means torturing and shaming Jesus. He not only blasphemed; He is a disgusting blasphemer."

Laughing with pleasure, they mocked, "His humiliating crown of thorns represents His true royalty."

The crowd's reviling meant to disgrace His pure heart, not simply accusing Him of working on the Sabbath or disobeying ceremonial law. Jesus never defended Himself or returned their curses. Instead, Jesus "turned those that hurdled insults at Him over to His Father Who judges all righteously." 1 Peter 2:23, Hebrews 12:3

We are powerfully struck by the physical pain of Jesus' death, but do we stop and consider the shame He carried?

He hung naked and bloody, in front of His family, friends and devoted followers. He knew His loved ones and disciples could only doubt every claim He asserted about Himself as He hung as an apparent fraud, able but not choosing to prove otherwise. Jesus knew more shame than we will ever know. All undeserved yet accepted.

We eagerly go to Christ's cross to remove our guilt for the three hours He hung there, taking our punishment. How much more should we also throw our shame on Christ? Being the Son of God, He lowered Himself to live as man, serve man, and die as a criminal. Just as Jesus shed His blood for the forgiveness of our sinning, Jesus died in disgrace as evidence to us that the disgraceful person that we see in the mirror was also placed on Him. Jesus paid for our shame, our feelings of worthlessness that admits, "I cannot forget how I cruelly damaged people with no regard. That's the pathetic me I am on the inside."

Taking our shame on Himself, He washes off our old identity as He give us His new identity. His Holy Spirit that dwells within us could no more live in harmony with shame than He could with guilt. 2 Corinthians 5:17, Hebrews 2:17, 9:23-26, 12:2

....

Arguably, not to throw our shame off of us and back onto its author devalues Christ's suffering on His cross in half. As we insult His work on the cross by hanging onto the guilt of past sins as if still unforgiven, we insult His cross by reclaiming shame.

Someone might ask, "I clearly see how Jesus took my punishment on His cross, so I get forgiveness. But how did Jesus take my shame and send it back to Satan?"

Ever hear someone say, "The people I trusted set me up as their scapegoat to coverup their huge screwup. They used me as their fall-guy."

We use the term "scapegoat" for someone who unjustly shoulders the blame of others. Wrongful behavior is placed onto an innocent party. Where does the term "scapegoat" originate from?

In the Old Testament, on the day of Atonement, God instructed Aaron to take two goats. Why two? Because each symbolized two very different truths that foreshadow Christ's cross.

The first goat was sacrificed on the altar to symbolize cleansing the Tabernacle. Picture the Tabernacle as a place where the nation's sins were deposited throughout the year as they made their animal sacrifices. After the worshippers offered their sacrifices for forgiveness throughout the year on the altar, they walked away cleansed *but their sins collected on the bloody altar.*

Over the course of the year the weight of those sins accumulated until, on the day of Atonement, Aaron's first goat was sacrificed to specifically cleanse the altar and entire Tabernacle. The sins of the prior year of the Jewish nation got wiped out, but when the next person offered their sacrifice, the sin bank got another "deposit." Leviticus 16:5-30

Jesus' death symbolized the sacrifice of the first goat. But Jesus, being infinite and sinless, cleansed all sins throughout time, not only for one nation or one year. John 1:29, 2 Corinthians 5:19, 1 John 2:2, 1 Timothy 2:2, 2 Peter 2:1, Hebrews 10:29

Now the puzzling part. *After the first goat was sacrificed, and the nation's sins are forgiven, what is left for Aaron to lay on the head of the scapegoat which is given the evil designation, to "Azazel?" And why not also sacrifice the scapegoat on the altar?*

Answer: Ownership of those sins is placed on the innocent scapegoat and then carried to Azazel in "dry places." Azazel is the true author, the title holder-he deserved his due.

This explains several things. Why the goat was not sacrificed, why it was sent far away, and where it was sent to.

As with the first goat, Aaron laid his hands on the scapegoat's head and pronounced all the sins of the nation. However, Aaron didn't sacrifice the scapegoat on the altar. This goat wasn't about cleansing of sin, it symbolized the taking away of their shame.

Simply put, although innocent, the scapegoat's job was to carry the ownership of all the evil committed by the Jews, out of the Tabernacle, then out of the camp, and finally back to sin's birthplace. Where shame was birthed. To remain with sin's conniving tempter that hides behind the curtain. Back to the deceiving liar who breaks all his promises. *Sin's originator.*

To go the distance, Aaron found a suitable man to take the scapegoat out of the entire Jewish community and far away to a dry "desolate place." There, the innocent goat carried the nation's shame to its true home address, never to find its way back to the Jewish camp. The desolate place referred to Satan's waterless home, where ownership for sin belongs, far-away from us and never to return. Matthew 12:43

The first goat performed the annual "deep cleaning" of the Tabernacle. The second goat removed all shame from those who committed those sins and carried that shame to Satan. Satan reaped the hell he sowed. The scapegoat symbolically had "Return shame to Sender" stamped on his head. Satan got his due.

As symbolized by the scapegoat, all our shame was placed on innocent Christ. Then, Christ carried our shame and left it at Satan's doorstep, never to come back to haunt us.

After placing all the nation's shame on the scapegoat, God didn't order Aaron to parade the scapegoat on a year-long excursion around the Jew's camp, yelling to the twelve tribes, "The good news is I sacrificed the first goat to remove your sins from the Tabernacle. So, we are all good there. But keep those sacrifices coming."

Then continuing, Aaron scolds, "The bad news is I am tying up this scapegoat in front of every tribe's camp to rub your nose in your shame all year. Feed it because you own it. Next month a neighboring tribe will feel the shame curse every day."

Christ's cross accomplishes once and for all time what the two goats symbolized. We are eternally forgiven for our sins, our temples are cleansed and indwelled by His Spirit, and shame is sent back to its rightful owner, Satan. Acts 13:35, 1 John 5:19, Colossians 1:13, Romans 5:19

……………..

There remains one colossal difference between Christ's cross and both goats. Jesus was resurrected. He left the shame due Satan and returned from death to life, giving us the authority to conquer the power of sin and shame in our lives.

Luke writes, "...He was not abandoned in Hades, and His flesh did not experience decay." Matthew 27:46, Acts 2:31, Hebrews 10:1-6

The animal sacrifices symbolically illustrated that innocent blood must be shed as a substitute to cleanse the guilty. No one could work off their offenses towards God, or sacrifice their own lives, not being innocent themselves.

In addition, no animal sacrifice ever possessed the power to bring themselves back to life. Animals only symbolized a substitute payment must be made by a blameless party. Only Jesus claimed to be the "Resurrection," possessing power over death. John 11:25

As Aaron's scapegoat represented taking the nation's shame back to Satan's doorstep, Jesus took on Himself our shame and left it on Satan's doorstep. Further, by His resurrection He conquered death, proving He possessed the ultimate power over sin's death-grip. In doing so, Jesus gave us power over sin's temptations while breathing and resurrection power over death itself.

Those who surrender their lives to Christ walk together with Him, as one, with no guilt or disgrace hovering over their heads. Matthew 20:18-28, Hebrews 2:10, 12:2, Zechariah 3:1-8, 12:10, John 14:26, 2 Corinthians 5:14-20

The sobering truth we now face, *"If we accept the ownership of shame or guilt, we diminish the work of Jesus' sacrifice."*

In essence, we retrieve the shame goat and make it our house pet. Harboring shame in our minds brings the scapegoat into our lives and defiles the Holy Spirit's temple. Abandoning our shame on Christ's cross for Him to carry away, leaves it at Satan's doorstep. Are we giving life to shame or guilt when Jesus conquered both? If so, we can't enjoy the oneness Jesus' cross provides for us. Romans 8:1, Psalms 16:10

....

In review, how do we understand the process of returning shame to its rightful owner?

We possess two defenses against Satan laying shame on our heads. First, our shame originates from our obedience to Satan. We obeyed him, blinded by his deceitful nature. Secondly, Jesus took our shame on His cross and then sent it back to its author. He left the curse in Satan's court, hades, where it came from.

Instead of Satan harassing us, we should go on the offensive, "Want to remind me of my foolishness while submitting to you? I dare you. I will make you will wish you never harassed me!" Acts 2:31

We transfer ownership of shame by taking every memory that triggers shame and humble down, "That was me under

Satan's management. I foolishly chose to trust in Satan, resisting obedience to Jesus. Clearly, I was headed for total disaster. But God's Spirit rescued me from Satan and my sin nature. I have a totally new identity. I am under new Management. God closed that book of horrors and opened a new book of life. Together we are writing a beautiful love story. Satan, and my flesh, and the world are all fired for failure to perform!" 2 Corinthians 7:11

"Now I love the joy of walking in selfless love. If I fall or think about my past, the Jesus in me picks me up, cleans me off, and heads me back to His place of peace. I know who I am now and where I belong and falling only reminds me of how painful serving Satan becomes. Shame-free with Jesus and shame-filled without Him."

"All that to say, Satan, when you try to put your hands on my head and rattle off all my sins, that is 'return shame to sender' time. *You are condemning yourself.* I am no longer your whipping boy. I no longer believe your lies regarding the inadequacy of Christ's cross and refuse to accept the shame He sent back to you. When you bring back disgraceful memories, they remind me of how thankful I am of my spotless life in Christ. And, I enjoy rubbing your face in your desolate world. Time to reap what you sowed."

....

What about the person who feels shame caused by the offenses done against them? As when a child is molested?

Or a spouse is cheated on? *Does Christ's cross remove innocent shame?*

Jesus felt the same disgrace as He heard the false accusations against His integrity and endured the suffering of their insults. All in front of His mother and loved ones. Jesus identifies with our burden of shame, shame we never deserved to carry. Philippians 2:1-11

Forgiveness claims, "If it isn't on Jesus' record, it isn't on my record." Shamelessness claims, "As Jesus took on Himself all shame, God finds no shame on me." At Christ's cross we unload our innocent shame and receive His stamp of blamelessness.

Listening to His endearing voice that corrects our rotten opinion of ourselves takes time and work. The process of overriding our shameful thoughts with God's loving heart and the truth of how He sees us draws us that much closer to the heart of God. Oneness.

Now Jesus walks proudly by our side, reminding us that shame no longer slimes our souls. His opinion of us overrides how we and others condemn us. Reputation, a meaningless man-centered notion, is replaced with God's opinion of us as He sees us through the work of Jesus' cross. Oneness with Christ grows as we realize His complete restoration. Psalms 22:6-8, 69:19,20, Hebrews 12:2

2

Humble Down

We might think that since we hold onto shame, and shame makes us feel miserable, it means we must hate ourselves. Is the answer, "I must learn to love myself?"

When we loathe someone, we thoroughly relish entertaining the worst for them. We snicker with satisfaction seeing the people we hate suffer. If hating ourselves is the reason we hold onto shame, we would snicker at our own pain, "Isn't this great fun feeling like a miserable failure?"

But we hate, not relish, going through shame's hell. That constitutes a strong indicator we hold onto shame for other reasons than hating ourselves.

Our injured pride holds onto our shame. We made embarrassing decisions, humiliating our pride. That is why shame causes us to hide our face from those who know our dirty secrets.

Proverbs 11:2 "When pride comes, then comes shame…"

Our shame originates from Satan's temptations to disobey God, but our shame sticks to us because we think highly of ourselves apart from God. "I hate how I embarrassed myself when I slept with…" Pride argues, "I want everyone to believe, me included, that I am a better person than that." When recalling ugly memories, our thinking highly of ourselves ignites shame.

In an attempt to cover our shame, our pride diverts our attention. We get rid of triggers or take a mind-altering substance to suppress it. Or we make noble sacrifices for others. And, of course, it helps to shift the blame on others.

Shame causes many believers to cringe when reading verses that list the fruits of the flesh, i.e., homosexuality, adultery, lying, stealing, gossip, murder, etc. Even though forgiven, they encounter many triggers that remind them of their bad history that they feel still represents the real them. "I think preachers enjoy ripping off old scabs. My 'hair trigger' shame would go if I could avoid reading those verses and getting pounded by oppressive morality messages ranting about the 'dirty dozen or the nasty nine.'"

Even when clearly understanding Christ's finished work to carry our shame away on His cross, if our "I am better than that really bad day" pride is never uncovered and repented of, we reason our shame is incurable until we work to redeem ourselves. We confess, "No one can re-write the past or erase a life-changing memory. It sticks to us. And triggers are inevitable. The damage is done. That ship has sailed. Time to volunteer at the soup kitchen until I feel better about myself." Or, we can do whatever distracts us to suppress our rotten memories.

If the gun isn't loaded, what difference does a "hair trigger" make? Memories of our dreadful past isn't our problem, our pride is.

Why not humble down and own who we are apart from obeying Christ in us? When walking in humility, we receive His gift of forgiveness and His freedom from shame.

Humility enables us to have a "come to Jesus" meeting. "Jesus, do I think more highly of myself than I ought to think?" "How could I act any differently than selfish without Your Spirit guiding me?" "Can I hang onto my pride and walk in freedom from shame?"

When we humble down, we realize it was us obeying Satan, not us on a bad day and we can somehow redeem ourselves. Jesus does all the redeeming, cleansing us of all our guilt and shame.

3

Party Killer

After we learn how God takes our haunting past and redeems it for His purposes, our disgusting past no longer shames us.

Paul, when Saul, tortured innocent Christians, yet he recounts those horrific days on several occasions. Paul turned his past evil into bragging on the power of God's grace. "…that I may know Him and the power of His resurrection…" Philippians 3:1-11, "…however for this reason I obtained mercy, that in me first Jesus Christ might show all longsuffering, as a pattern to those who are going to believe…" 1 Timothy 1:15, Acts 26:10,11

We too can take our ugly past and joyfully rub Satan's nose in God's grace. Then, after sending shame back to its rightful author, we focus on loving God back. 2 Corinthians 2:16

The following word picture illustrates the difference between making a pet of a shame goat or accepting the freedom that Christ's cross paid for. Imagine these two different endings to the parable of the Prodigal Son in Luke 15.

Jesus starts the story with the younger son asking for his inheritance early. Upon receiving it, he promptly leaves home to party in a foreign country. After losing everything through reckless living and dishonoring his father's name, he drags himself home, in disgrace and starving. He only hopes to work and eat with the servants.

His father sees him coming far off and runs out to meet him. Without a scolding, he gives his wayward son a symbolic family ring, a coat of honor, and sandals. All items that express acceptance, not shame. Then comes the huge feast to celebrate His son coming home.

Now the first scenario of the prodigal son at the feast:

The reckless son, sitting next to his father, stands up and acknowledges, "I am utterly embarrassed sitting up here. What a nightmare. I cannot believe I was so irresponsible. I lost everything. I even stooped to feeding pigs. It haunts me to think I made so many foolish decisions. I know better."

With a heavy sigh, he meekly confesses, "Please forgive me. I deserve servant status, at least until I prove myself responsible. I am unworthy of this ring, coat and sandals and I need to take them off. I know what I think of me, and I definitely know what my brother thinks of me, and probably what most of you think of me."

He then concluded, looking for a little sympathy, "Etched vividly into my memory are the atrocious things I did and *that were done to me. I learned the hard way that no one truly cared for my well-being but they did love my money. I will accept living as a servant in my father's home. I will work hard until I remove the utter disgrace I am to myself and my family."*

Now the second scenario:

The reckless son stands up and announces, "I am humbled and stand in complete awe. It was my foolishness, living apart from my father, that made a miserable mess of my life. Even though I ran away as soon as my father gave me my inheritance, upon my return my father instantly gave me my sonship back."

Tearfully, he continues, "My father embraced my filthy body and called me his son. My amazing father eagerly forgave my rebellion that injured his heart and brought shame to his name."

"I want to confess my unthinkable rebellion to reveal just how gracious my father's heart is. He ran to me full of joy, I walked to him full of shame. I smelled like pigs yet he hugged and kissed me. He never rebuked me for my foolishness or disrespect. Instead, my awesome father held me tight, as if I was the son he always wanted."

"I know what I think of me, what my brother thinks of me, and what most of you think of me. But, I only care what my father thinks of me because I want to make him happy."

Gesturing to his father, "I want to propose a toast to the most forgiving and loving father in the world... with an incredible ability to forget! And, if anyone is considering running off to a foreign land, I can assure you that you are heading for disaster. Underneath the love and guidance of my terrific father is where you want to stay."

Neither son forgot their evil actions in their rebellion, but only one remained haunted by their behavior.

In the first scenario the son made it about how his behavior belittled himself. He thought he could live at a higher moral level without his father. His injured pride prohibited him from accepting his father's reinstatement into the family. He relied on his estimation of his own opinion and other's opinions of his worthiness, not his father's opinion.

The son in the first scenario came back no different than he left. Instead of broken and thankful to be alive, he was full of self-confidence, disabling him from receiving an unearned gift from his father.

Pride caused his continued shame. And his pride kept him from realizing how gracious his father was in forgiving him. Imagine his father's thoughts while he whined about his painful past? "He wants to live in the past when I offer him complete freedom and blessings. He wallows in the shame I released before he even committed his offenses. His pride is his curse, 'I can prove I deserve better than pig food. I can clear my own name. Hold off on making me right.'" 1 Timothy 4:10

The son in the second scenario humbled down and realized that apart from his father, he could only act like a fool. Further, in his humility, he could receive his father's unearned gifts. In regard to his family standing, he agreed with his father to bless his father.

In the second scenario the humble son focused on the praise that his father deserved. He only referred to his evil behavior to magnify his father's forgiveness. "If my father can forgive me of my treacherous behavior, he can forgive anyone, because I am the greatest of sinners."

The second scenario brings glory to God with no guilt or shame sticking to the son. This son had no need or desire to forget his ugly past. No fear of triggers. Remembering only brings greater gratitude and glory to his father's kindness. To remind him of his past gets him preaching how much he loves his forgiving and forgetful father. Romans 2:4

The entire second scenario pivots on one decision. "Whose opinion of me will I choose?" If I proudly choose mine, I will grieve my kindhearted father and throw a wet blanket on His coming home party. If I refuse to grieve my Father any longer, I will choose His verdict and enjoy the party.

Christ's redemption means far more than "zeroing out our sin in God's record books." He changes us on the inside, implanting His Spirit and calling us His children. The Father sees us no differently than He sees His own Son. Jesus makes us completely holy, not a forgiven but "decrepit child" that still embarrasses God. Ephesians 1:5

4

Wallowing In Shame

Not every believer wants to know how to overcome shame. Guilt and shame are great companions to keep around if someone needs a handy excuse to play the victim. "I simply can't forget the terrible things that I have done. I know God forgives me, but I can't live with myself until I restore my self-worth. Please understand my emotional torture...and that beatdown is why I drink too much..."

Why did Jesus first ask the lame man, "Do you want to get well?" Answer: Responsibilities come with being well. John 5:6

If we rehearse our shame or hear others wallow in theirs, we need to humble down and side with God's heart in the matter. How would we feel if we rescued someone from an appallingly abusive relationship yet all they talk about is their past foolishness, "How could I be so stupid?" "Why did I give them my best years." "I am embarrassed that I was manipulated by their narcissistic nonsense."

Instead of living in the present, enjoying their freedom, they continue to whip their own backs. The slavery continues, self-inflicted.

Or, when triggers cause us to remember our past, do we make the "feast" about celebrating Jesus' love for us, not disgusting Him by casually rehearsing the repulsive things we did when choosing our abuser over Him? Do we keep a high opinion of His opinion towards our restoration, and rest knowing He set us free? He makes us family, not our self-worth. Do we keep a low opinion of who we are apart from Christ? We state to the world of His love and forgiveness and how they too can be free of guilt and shame. Duet. 7:7-10

....

Our Christian walk does not stop at overcoming shame. Believers must produce selfless love to enjoy oneness with Christ. "Oneness grows on the other side of obedience." Galatians 5:22-24, 1 John 1:7

On a sobering note, 1 John 2:28 states that we are to "…abide in Him, that when He appears, we may have confidence and not be ashamed before Him at His coming." If we do not abide in Him, we can expect to be ashamed. This shame sticks to us because Jesus died to make us holy but we resisted walking out what He has worked in, His selfless love. 1 John 4:17

As the son in the second scenario at the feast, how can we not humble down, confess our faults, then receive and share His love with a world burdened by guilt and shame?

Which brings up a few more obvious questions:

How can anyone who learns what Christ went through to remove their sin and shame, as far as the east is from the west, enjoy or even allow mental "air time" to their prior relationships filled with rebellion? Who could worship God's amazing grace and allow triggers of old shameful behaviors to turn into entertaining that behavior again? How disrespectful for us to aggrandize our pig slop at His feast? Psalms 103:12, Isaiah 43:25, Micah 7:18

When we attempt to prove ourselves worthy, we build with wood, hay, and stumble. All burn. When we are grateful, He makes us worthy, and we endeavor to love Him back with His selfless love. 1 Corinthians 3:11-17, John 17:23

In Summary:

Many Christians remain tortured by their shame because they wrongly believe that Christ's cross forgave their sins but Jesus failed to take away the disgrace of the person they once were and then change who they are now.

They act like a person running out of a courtroom, proclaiming, "Jesus announced He forgave me of my horrific offences and I am released! No hellhole prison for me!"

But as they leave the courthouse, they squint their eyes to avoid seeing the faces of the people they wounded. They cocoon up to avoid the triggers that remind them of the disgusting things they did. They believe that the same person that walked into the courtroom and committed those horrifying actions still represents who they are. They ran out "fresh clean snow covering stinking manure." Self-loathing reflects the proper attitude for what lies on the inside of the sickening person who committed those evil acts, forgiven or not.

The solution...

They rushed out before the Judge made a far grander announcement. After the Judge declared, "I find the defendant innocent of all charges," He removed His judicial robe, and stepped in as their new Father, announcing their new identity, "It gives Me great pleasure to adopt this innocent child as My own. They will only be identified under My name from now on. I see them no differently than I see Jesus."

Now they walk out of the courthouse under a different name than they walked in with. The name of Jesus, with His sinless and shameless nature representing who they are on the inside.

But how do they reconcile their memories of their criminal actions?

They don't need to pretend those actions were beneath them. Or make up a false alibi. Or blameshift. Jesus took everyone's rap sheet and plead guilty. The Father, as Judge, found His Son guilty of all of them. Then, after Christ's cross, when the Father reviews the incident report, we are no longer on the list. We go by a new name now, not our old name, the person found at the scene of the crime. Romans 8:15-17, Ephesians 1:5, 4:24

We don't deny our actions while living in our "foreign" land, we denounce our citizenship there. "On my own, I am a sleazeball. Satan ate me for lunch. But when I renounced my citizenship to that foreign land, my criminal history and shame went with it because all my sins and shame was carried by Christ on His cross. Only by God's grace I am alive physically and spiritually. Only by God adopting me into His family am I able to stand shame free." John 1:9, Romans 1:21, 2:14-15

Not walking in the freedom of Christ's cross, we wear shame like a persistent headache. We learn Biblical truths, but our subtle pride fools us into ignoring several glaring contradictions. Holding onto shame is unwittingly confessing:

Living in oneness with Jesus includes our shame. Shame coexists with perfect love. Essentially, we are foolishly confessing, "Jesus, I still suffer shame because You didn't suffer enough shame on Your cross as the crowds mocked and spit on You."

We believe our old nature, simply because we remember our offenses, still paints a truer picture of who we are than our new Christ implanted born-again nature. How arrogant and inconsiderate to bring that pig slop to the party Jesus throws on our behalf.

We keep a high opinion of ourselves, thinking we can still make up for our embarrassing moral failures. We reason we must we redeem ourselves or our shame is rightfully ours. We keep a low opinion of Christ's completed work because it offends our pride.

We wrongly assume our shame slipped past Christ's cross. We fail to realize that Christ's death and resurrection destroyed the power of sin and shame over us, but not their nagging temptations to believe their destructive lies. The one we choose to obey, either His voice or our haunting memories, embraces the one we love. *We don't lack for willpower when we listen to shame and guilt. We lack for love for the Master of the Ceremony.*

We imagine that Jesus makes room for shameful thoughts when walking in fellowship with Him. "Jesus, excuse me while I mentally rehearse all the revolting things Satan and I did together. I don't intend on repeating any of them, just going down memory lane with my old party buddy."

Incredibly, we assume the absurd notion that God planned for His peace and joy in our lives to co-exist with our shame. ETC.

Shame destroys our lives. Sometimes due to ignorance, oftentimes pride's doing. Take God's heart in the matter. How could our regurgitating our shame in His presence not grieve God, possibly even more than our offense committed when first walking away from Him to a foreign land?

By clutching onto the shame Jesus took on His cross, we neglect the full work of Christ's cross.

Refusing to humbly accept our new name and identity, we trust our arrogant opinion of who we are now, based on who we were, over God's Word and new work in our lives. *If we walked out what He worked in, we witness undeniable proof of our new identity.* Colossians 2:10, 2 Corinthians 5:19-21, Ezekiel 11:19, Ephesians 4:22-24

Will we humble down, have a "come to Jesus" meeting, and ask God how He sees us? Then, will we agree? Every time our past wants to haunt us, will we take that shame attempt and ask Christ, "Are You the One bringing up my past to rub my nose in it?" And, "Do I see me as You see me, or do I see me apart from the work of Your cross?" And, "I want to thank You that I am not that person anymore and that You also carried my shame on Your cross." Plus, "I see the fruit of Your Spirit in my life. Thanks for redeeming my old ugly heart into one that pleases You. How can I please You next?"

In regards to the injured person who innocently assumed shame, they too must ask Jesus, "Do You see me as guilty?" And, "Have I forgiven the person who hurt me, leaving them in Your merciful hands?" "Do my victim thoughts honor You?" "What attitude do You choose for me towards …?" James 1:5

Part Two:
Freedom in Christ

Jesus often used stories to illustrate His truths. This section addresses many overlooked Biblical truths, using stories as helpful word pictures.

5

Selfishness Strangles Freedom

Opening Thoughts

Without drawing attention to itself, our self-serving nature is always making "backroom deals" in our minds. When choosing to help someone, our minds first weigh if they will respond properly. "I will consider doing something nice for them, but are they likely to do something nice in return?" Or, "If I hold up my end of the deal, they better hold up their end." We judge relationships based on how well they work for us. Our hearts have a nagging "return address" attached on all of our goodness. "There must be a give-and-take or this won't work."

Our self-absorbed birth nature even puts a return address on our good works with God. "If I change the way I live, will You get me out of this mess?" Or, "I gave You my life, tell me life gets better than this for me?"

Many claim they are in a committed relationship but their self-serving nature seduces them to look around to evaluate whether another person might offer more. Maybe they dream about "the one who got away." Self-love longs to have better and carefully evaluates if it's worth the costs.

In the end, selfishness can only create shallow and broken relationships, not God's quality of unbreakable oneness.

Selfishness causes our anxiety, anger, and discontentment. What else but selfishness drives someone nuts when striving to get what they want? And what makes someone depressed when things don't work out as planned? What causes someone to get angry when treated unfairly? Selfishness. Does that sound like selfishness makes your life better, even if in a 50/50 relationship?

Selfishness hinders oneness, the incredible life we were meant to enjoy when obeying the nature of God within us. We were built to run on His selfless love and experience oneness with God and others. When we obey His selfless love, we will love freely and we will absolutely love our lives. Anxiety turns to peace, anger to love, and depression to hope.

Anne's Story: Part One

Anne was loved, incredibly lovely, but as lovable as dead possum. By age sixteen her body looked like it belonged to a twenty-one-year-old model. And judging from her skimpy wardrobe, Anne's favorite color was olive, her skin tone. Naturally athletic and with a strong will to win, year after year Anne walked away with the MVP trophy in her volleyball league. With her beauty, shapely figure, and natural athleticism, Anne's peers put up with her self-absorbed attitude, giving her no reason but to believe she reigned as the queen of her world.

Thinking herself as "Queen Anne," she disrespected every authority that contested her queenship. Every authority but one: her straight-shooting volleyball coach, Mrs. Cato.

When getting into the front seat of Coach Cato's car, on the way to a volleyball game, Anne's first words to her coach mocked her father's parting instructions, "Remember Anne, come home right after the game to study." Anne continued by sarcastically mimicking his earlier directions, "Anne, you need to eat right to stay healthy. Anne, you only hurt yourself when you stay up late talking on the phone or on social media. Anne, if you dress like that boys are…blah, blah, blah." Anne then paused and added, "My father is a tyrant. First he tells me he loves me and then he beats me down with his endless expectations. What he calls parenting, I call suffocation."

Coach Cato, remembering her own childhood, replied, "Yeah, I grew up without a dad. Do you think I should be thankful my mom was rarely in my business? Her only expectation for me was not to make trouble for her."

"Well, at least she accepted you for the way you wanted to be. I think my dad has a psycho twin. First my nice dad thanks me for cleaning up the kitchen, but then his evil twin bosses me around. 'You really shouldn't wear that. Are you treating others with respect?' It never ends!"

Anne's voice turned irate, "Tell me that isn't twisted? My good dad is easy to please. My psycho dad is a harsh dictator."

Coach Cato followed up on Anne's little tirade with a few questions. "So, what upsets you is that your dad is pleased easily when you obey in small ways, but then he puts higher expectations on you?"

"Heck yeah! When my dad piles on his ridiculous expectations, it turns into cruelty."

"Hang on, Anne," Coach Cato strongly interjected, "so you admit your dad's hard expectations are really for your own good. You don't mind tolerating the easy stuff, but you push back when he asks you to do anything you think is unreasonable. Or, you will throw a 'don't mess with the queen' hissy fit."

Anne didn't give an inch. "All I want is my freedom to forge my own path. To live my life my way."

"Ok, let's look at this from a different angle," Coach Cato reasoned. "Suppose we play a really talented team and they start killing us. So, I give the whole team the freedom to play however they wanted. No guidelines, just do your thing."

"We would lose and you would be a joke of a coach and get your butt fired. End of story."

"Ok, so suppose I teach everyone stick to the rules of the game. And, I give positive remarks for simple things like remembering the rotation and hitting the ball using the correct technique. But then, to save us from losing, I bark at you and explain why you missed a hard shot. So, I am easily pleased on one hand, demanding perfection on the other. Am I psycho?"

"I can see where this is going…"

"Yeah, Anne," Coach Cato's voice grew stronger, "maybe Queen Anne is talking crazy. What makes me a winning coach, makes me a cruel tyrant by your thinking."

"You missed it by a mile, Coach," Anne returned, still sarcastic. "The huge difference is I volunteered for your abuse because I want to win. But I don't want to win at anything my prudish dad thinks is important."

"Really, Anne?" Coach Cato replied. "You just made winning a stupid game more important than your life's future. Anyway, a good parent has no choice but to prepare their child for life's hard challenges. You want your dad to let you blaze your own trail right off a cliff."

"Well, frankly Coach, what you call a cliff I call a pothole. And wherever my dad wants to direct me, I don't want to go there."

"So, this isn't really about your dad being pyscho, or unloving, or even wrong. This is about you wanting to be your own boss, no matter how stupid it gets and how witchy you have to be."

Unphased by her coach's remarks, Anne smiled and repeated, "Witchy, huh? What's the matter, Coach? Afraid to use the 'B' word around a student?"

Getting a disgusted look from her coach, Anne quickly brought the conversation back on point. "All I want is to be my own boss. Having that freedom alone is winning. I am not that stupid to think I'm so smart that I won't hit a few potholes along the way. Oh well. A price I am willing to pay. But I am smart enough to keep my party under control."

"You want to take your chances…that is your call. But I am warning you, potholes often turn into cliffs. However, you and I both know that all that whining about your dad being pyscho because he places hard expectations on you is nonsense."

"Well, bottom line, my dad makes me feel like I am drowning, not like the ruling queen of the world. I am not interested in working hard to get whatever stupid carrot he dangles as a reward. He just needs to back off and let me stumble my way through life."

Coach Cato realized the school they were to play was just ahead. She quickly recounted, "So, your argument is, 'Get out of my face, Dad, unless you want to give the queen your money to help blaze her own trail even faster off the cliff that she refuses to believe is there'?"

"That works for me. Win or lose, it is my life and I want to live it my way. But for now, and only because I want to win, which means I am still the queen, I will put up with your tough coaching."

Coach Cato turned off the engine and sarcastically wrapped up their conversation. "Well, this is a tough call. Soooo hard to tell who is loving and who is a rude witch? You are a big fish in a tiny pond. One day, that will change."

Easy to Please, Hard to Satisfy

God is easy to please in the same way a mother (or father) tirelessly pours out love on a newborn baby. Although physically exhausted and often awake much of the night, the mother's nurturing continually flows out with no regard for her child's inability to pay her back or even being capable of comprehending how much love their frail state requires. Just holding her newborn brings her great joy!

As her child grows, a loving mother is easily elated by her baby's jovial laugh. She takes videos of her child's barely intelligible first words and when she watches her little toddler's first steps.

When her child gets a couple of years older, the mother no longer is thrilled at baby steps or slurred words. Because she loves her child, she places higher "hard to satisfy" expectations on her child. She expects her child to speak in sentences and learn to run.

In addition to placing loving expectations on a child, a mother doesn't hesitate to pull the steak knife from her child's hand, regardless of the hissy fit that follows. Her love doesn't fear the tantrum that her child's controlling attitude throws because she is more concerned about her child's welfare than her child's inability to comprehend the love that drives her parenting decisions.

It's our inborn self-serving nature that insists on being in control in order to make self-serving decisions. Any authority that jeopardizes our ability to reign as king or queen of our domains, that pulls the knife out of our hand, is fought because they prevent us from making self-ruled decisions. Control is a means to an end, living for ourselves.

Spiritually, how is God's heart easy to please? Take Jesus' story of the prodigal son. All the wayward son had to do was humbly walk home after he squandered his inheritance. His father ran out to him and then threw a huge party. We walk, God runs. Christ offers forgiveness for simply believing in Him. He doesn't first require a probationary period or impressive good works (Luke 15:11-32; John 1:12).

Given the incredible sacrifice Christ made to bring us into a place of oneness with Him, and how little the world appreciates His sacrifice, it is evident God willingly and knowingly overspent His costly love on the world. But when an individual simply turns from walking the path alone and yields to God, thousands of angels get up and dance, revealing heaven's easy to please heart (Luke 15:22; First Timothy 2:3-4; First John 2:2).

On God's side of the equation, He gave the price of His Son. On our side, we submit one baby step at a time to His leading and He is pleased. "For whoever gives you a cup of water to drink in My name, because you belong to Christ, assuredly, I say to you, he will by no means lose his reward" (Mark 9:41).

How is God's heart hard to satisfy? God knows that selfishness, to any degree, destroys our lives. God will not stop parenting us with high expectations until our love is purified of all its selfishness. Out of love for us, He necessarily prunes even the branches that bear fruit, to help them bear more fruit (John 15:2).

God lays out many difficult expectations to utterly destroy selfishness, such as "overcome evil with good" (Romans 12:21), "let each esteem others better than himself" (Philippians 2:3), "sell what you have and give to the poor" (Matthew 19:21), and "not come to be served, but to serve" (Matthew 20:28).

God's hard to satisfy expectations top out at "be perfect, just as your Father in heaven is perfect" (Matthew 5:48). In essence, "God will not stop maturing us into His children, spending His selfless love on others." As we mature, we will absolutely love our journey walking with in harmony with Him. With His love pouring through us, loving the naturally unlovable becomes our first nature.

Until then, any selfishness that hinders oneness must mercilessly be cut out as though it was a cancer that will destroy us. God acquiescing to a partially rebellious heart would be unloving and sells short the work of Christ's cross.

In time, and on the other side of our obedience, God's hard to satisfy expectations become a liberating source of freedom from the bondage that our selfishness brings on us. Obedience to God's selfless nature grows to feel like a soft pillow to rest our exhausted hearts on. "Therefore if the Son makes you free, you shall be free indeed" (John 8:36).

A bit more about our elusive birth nature.

As stated, the long-fought argument, whether mankind is born basically good or evil, begins with the wrong two options. The true options are actually between selfish or selfless. Which is it?

Why does the government continually make countless laws? Why must the government tax us to distribute help to the needy? Why are the courts and prisons jammed? Why do we keep everything we own locked and alarmed? Why do we pay for protection from spyware? Why do stores have cameras? Why do we have so many attorneys, wars, psychologists, divorce, etc.? Why expensive armies? What drives our fears, anger, coveting, and jealousy?

Obviously, we are born with our hearts hell-bent on selfishness. Nonetheless, the confusion comes from equating "selfish" with only evil. Anyone can choose to act good while living for themselves.

Many wisely choose doing good things for selfish reasons. Why not be kind if you will be treated kindly in return? Why not work hard to get ahead? Why not be honest if it pays you to be honest? Delayed gratification and self-control are fantastic self-serving attitudes to possess to improve one's domain (Matthew 5:46-47).

Most counseling, both secular and even "Christian," appeals to how choosing good over evil behavior will better serve our selfishness.

"If you give your spouse what they want, they will return the favor."

"How is that behavior working for you?"

Rarely do counselors address the choice between selfish and selfless. Smart selfishness gets far more return customers because our birth nature naturally agrees.

Could you imagine a counselor advising, "You need to show kindness, whether or not it comes back to you." Or, "Stop making decisions based on how they will profit you. Ask God what serves Him." And, "Do something helpful for the person that just hurt you, simply to please God." Those statements are very offensive to the king or queen who already feels violated, the very reason why they are talking to the counselor in the first place.

Source matters. Our selfish nature produces a quality of love that destroys our lives and hinders our walk with Christ. To change our nature, our "want to," we require a new Ruler. We need Christ to implant His selfless nature within us, which is the fuel we use to live on, making us one with Him and others.

"Every way of a man is right in his own eyes, but the Lord weighs the hearts" (Proverbs 21:2).

"Most assuredly, I say to you, unless one is born again, he cannot see the kingdom of God" (John 3:3).

6

Recognize Your Enemy

Opening Thoughts

God is a God of choice. He never destroys our will. The question is whose will does our will choose to serve? Our own will or God's will?

The decision we make is not determined by whose will has more power. Love decides. If we choose to obey God's will, we love serving Him and His kingdom. If we choose to obey our own will, we love serving ourselves and building our own kingdom or queendom. Once God opens our eyes to understanding this choice, us verses Him, the choice we make embraces the one we love. Nothing more, nothing less (Matthew 6:24).

Then, after choosing whose will to serve, we place ourselves in what feels like "lower heaven" or "upper hell." Like appetizers whet your appetite for the upcoming meal, we order up a taster of heaven or hell here and now. We taste samples of peace or anxiety, love or intolerance, patience or annoyance, giving or taking, contentment or coveting, oneness or division, hope or depression. "Oh, taste and see that the Lord is good" (Psalm 34:8).

Our hearts decide, yielded to or resisting the Spirit of Christ within. The samples of upper hell or lower heaven are tasted by all. Jesus reminds us in John 16:8 that the Holy Spirit "will convict the world of sin, and of righteousness, and of judgment" (see also Jeremiah 17:9-10 and Romans 2:5-16).

Anne's Story: Part Two

As expected, Anne stood out in her performance. She rallied her team from a sure loss while she attracted the lustful desires of everyone in the gym that didn't shave their legs. She couldn't wait to relish in her MVP show on the way home.

"So, did Queen Anne show up or what?"

Coach Cato ignored her gloating. "Because you listened to my corrections, instead of whining about how hard they were."

Anne smelled a rat. "I was hoping to enjoy my awesomeness for a little while before you pound me with some nauseating life lesson."

Overlooking Anne's little glory party, Coach Cato continued, "You only enjoyed victory because you didn't let Queen Anne on the court. You played as a team working together, taking my advice on how to win against a difficult opponent." Coach Cato chuckled, "Queen Anne must have been locked up in the dungeon."

"You're wrong. The queen was only holding her breath until the game was over. Then, she gets back on her throne and demands, 'Bow down losers.'"

Anne paused and pointing her finger at her coach, added, "I know where you want to go with this, but you forget. I don't want to win at my dad's game. Heck, my hotness would be embarrassed to win. Sorry Coach, no connection."

"Not so fast, your 'hotness.' You just admitted that you had to shut down the queen to win on the court. I am telling you the queen will ruin your life off the court. She will weaken all your relationships and make your life miserable."

"And another thing about your 'queenship,'" Coach Cato continued. "Sooner or later she will get her butt kicked and your 'hotness' will turn into your 'trampness.' You will be embarrassed to live in your own skin."

Anne cut in, "And you say I'm overdramatic? I just want to enjoy my life. For that, I need the freedom to make my own decisions. I will take my chances on where my choices take me. I'm not afraid of cliffs."

"You only think you are fearless. You're are afraid of your self-absorbed queen not getting what she wants and losing the power to make it happen. One day, you will learn that control is just a myth and trying to live for yourself brings never ending stress to deal with."

Anne repeated her coach, "So, you think Queen Anne fears taking off her crown because she is a selfish control freak? It has nothing to do with my father actually ruining my life?"

Coach Cato agreed, "Yeah. And, Queen Anne is completely obnoxious. You think the world serves you. So, you don't have any real friends."

"Well," Anne responded shaking her head, "you can stop the shrink session because I don't fear anything but turning out like my dad. And, true or not true, I love the feeling of the queen being in charge. So far, life is great."

Coach Cato pulled into a juice shop to buy a couple of smoothies. As they walked in, a filthy homeless man stood at the door, begging for money. On their way out, Coach Cato asked the homeless man, "Would you like to stay in my travel trailer? No one else is using it. We'd make sure you get regular meals, and you could help out with a few ranch jobs?"

"Lady, do I look like I want someone to tell me when to get up and tell me what to do, and then choose what I eat? I am the boss of my life and no one tells me what to do. Unlike you, I am free and I love it." Irritated, he then stuck out his hand, "Are you going to give me a buck or not?"

Anne and Coach Cato got back into the car and drove home. Neither spoke a word, but "trampness" kept ringing in Anne's ear.

Right Choices, Wrong Motives

"Crown" wearers often experience success. As stated, our selfish nature still chooses between good or evil to serve. Noble or ignoble. When the queen or king uses wisdom and self-control to govern their domains, they personally benefit. Why not be kind, honest, orderly, fair, law-abiding, hardworking, and gracious? Honey produces better results than vinegar.

Those who employ honorable character qualities while living independent of God's rule do so with selfish ends in mind. Noble character is chosen to better increase and control their domains. "I will treat my neighbor kindly because I may need the favor returned." "Either be honest now or risk the chance of getting fired." "I must stay faithful to my spouse or I will lose half of what I own." *When someone is honest or kind because it pays them to be, they cease to truly be honest or kind.*

Without a heart yielded to God, self-driven "good" operates with strings attached. If others do not respond appropriately to their kindness, upper hell creeps in—frustration, anger, and feelings of being cheated and outplayed.

Wrong Choices with Wrong Motives

And then there are those who foolishly employ evil to manage their domains. They take far more than they give, impulsively make emotional decisions, cheat, use half-truths or anger to manipulate, and break the law. Upper hell usually comes in like a flood: job loss, divorce, legal and criminal issues, financial difficulties, constantly looking over their shoulders, trying to remember the lies used, etc.

If they learn from their life management mistakes, they wisely convert to using honey instead of vinegar and patiently wait to get what they want. *Few may realize, out of their continued frustration to please their insatiable selfishness, they need a new ruler inside, not new management techniques.*

……………….

Upper hell, anger, fear, and self-pity blanket our planet like swamp gas and very few seem to take notice. Why? In order to remain self-ruled, a degree of upper hell becomes an "acceptable loss." When using noble qualities for selfish reasons, the losses should be less, but nonetheless unavoidable. The demands of maintaining and improving one's domain promise stress, fear, distrust, loneliness, anger, depression, discontentment, and a myriad of other emotions indicative of hell, and everyone just puts up with the whole lot. We become "bondage blind" like we become "nose blind" to an odor that we have grown accustomed to.

How often do we hear statements such as, "Closing this big contract is making me sick"? "How are we going to pay our credit card payment?" "I need to get smashed tonight." "Is he cheating on me?"

In contrast, remember the words of Jesus when He said, "Do not lay up for yourselves treasures on earth, where moth and rust destroy and where thieves break in and steal; but lay up for yourselves treasures in heaven" (Matthew 6:19-20).

In summary, the person that lives self-serving in their relationships will face several inescapable and miserable enslavements.

Self-serving people ask, "Am I giving more than I am getting? Can I do better? Should I dump my partner for a better-looking partner?" Fighting and distrust inevitably results. After experiencing the bitter sting of one or two failed relationships, the next relationship is entered into with walls up around their heart. Their lips may say, "I love you," but their hearts and minds remain guarded and distrusting. Consequently, relationships remain paper thin. "Friends with benefits" is the safe place where one's need for sexual intimacy meets self-preservation. Oneness is lost to selfishness and written off as an elusive dream.

Additionally, self-serving people naturally suspect others of thinking like themselves. Every encounter gravitates to the level of selfishness that is pre-existing in themselves.

For example, indifferent people project their indifference on others. "They arrived late because they really don't care, not because of their lousy 'traffic' excuse."

Or, takers assume, "Everyone is out to get something from me. I need to protect my stuff. The way I spell 'trust' is s-t-u-p-i-d." Manipulators wonder, "Are they complementing me just to get me to say or do something for them later?" Everyone a self-serving person deals with becomes suspect to being the very fraud they are themselves.

Because a self-serving person projects their ugly heart onto others, they not only suffer from the anxiety and anger of their own selfishness, but they project that emotional bondage onto everyone like a spreading cancer. Selfishness colors their entire world ugly.

Paul tells us in Titus 1:15-16, "To the pure all things are pure, but to those who are defiled and unbelieving nothing is pure; but even their mind and conscience are defiled" (see also Matthew 7:1-5 and Romans 2:1-4).

Perhaps the most irritating enslavement of the self-consumed king or queen constitutes the constant comparing and competing of kingdoms. Kings and queens endlessly evaluate themselves compared to the domains of others. "How does my little world measure up? Am I as attractive, smart, rich, talented, sexy, promising, and strong? Is my little empire looking slummy? Embarrassing? Do I need to strive to improve my cheesy domain to gain my self-esteem back? Is it even possible? I think another trip to the refrigerator will kill the pain."

Paul states in Second Corinthians 10:12, "But they, measuring themselves by themselves, and comparing themselves among themselves, are not wise" (see also Proverbs 20:6 and Romans 12:3).

7

Love Decides

Opening Thoughts

A great deal is misunderstood about the battle in our minds as we pursue walking in oneness with God. We don't need to get smarter to overcome lying, stealing, coveting, fighting, etc. *Information doesn't war.* Everyone knows from their own experience that clearly knowing the right thing to do does not mean you will choose the right thing. Our minds calculate the facts. "I know the cost of this new car is far more than my budget can afford," but then we say, "Who cares. I love it!" Where then is the battle fought?

The "greatest commandment" orders the chain of command for our decision making: from the heart, to the mind, and then to the body.

"You shall love the Lord your God with all your heart, with all your soul, and with all your mind" (Matthew 22:37). Also, Deuteronomy 6:5, Mark 12:30

As your arm doesn't move unless your mind tells it to, your mind simply responds to your heart's love decisions. Information travels both directions, but our decisions originate from our hearts.

We get confused about the verses that state we must "transform our mind" and "renew our mind." But are our minds the source of our problem? *There are also verses that say, "do not steal" and "do not lie." Are our hands and lips the source of our problem? Of course not.* "From out of the heart the mouth speaks" (Matthew 15:18). Romans 12:1,2, Ephesians 4:17-20

The heart makes the primary decision, the mind agrees and does the "math." The body then knows what to do to accomplish the heart's desires.

The truth of the matter is the battle is fought in your heart and the choice your heart makes establishes the one it loves. Jesus said there is no second place in love. No consolation prize for coming in second. Spiritually, love chooses only one at the exclusion of any other. The loser is rejected with a strong bias because the two choices remain bitter enemies.

"No one can serve two masters; for either he will hate the one and love the other, or else he will be loyal to the one and despise the other" (Matthew 6:24).

Our second error constitutes our watering down the word "love." We have diminished love to mean little or nothing.

Someone may passionately announce, "I would love to be slim and fit," but if they often sit on the couch and eat potato chips, then their heart is actually saying, "Just kidding. I really love being lazy and eating junk food!" A college student may say to all their friends, "I would love to be a doctor," but if they play video games instead of studying, then their heart is truly saying, "I'm just dreaming. I really love gaming."

The choice you make is the one you love and your heart makes the call, not some battle of confusion in one's mind that must be renewed in order to put down the potato chips.

Our love for God decides our obedience. Jesus declared in John 14:23, "If anyone loves Me, he will keep My word." Now, if we casually use the word "love" the same way with God as we do with being slim and fit, God says we don't really love Him (because we don't). *This distinction matters because we can't fault our disobedience on a lack of understanding or willpower. Our will wins every time. Love makes the call. If we sin, we have a greater love for something other than God. Love never does what it hates. Romans 8:12*

God will not ignore our other loves that we choose above loving Him. Being lovingly hard to satisfy, He will continue to prune away areas in our selfish hearts, as painful as it may be to us (grab the knife from our hands). The payoff comes after we obey His leading. Our experience of His love becomes so pure and real to us that His love ultimately ruins us for all other competing loves. Along the way, He succors us with rich tidbits of who He is.

Anne's Story: Part Three

Coach Cato dropped Anne off and managed to hurry home in time to get a mountain bike ride in before dark. Coach enjoyed working out her pent-up emotions from the game with an exhausting ride up the steep mountain roads behind her ranch. After changing into her brightly colored biking clothes, she clipped her riding shoes into the bike pedals and started on her strenuous ride.

While she was pedaling deep in thought, an oncoming truck suddenly lost control as it veered across the road. To avoid getting killed, Coach Cato swerved her bike off the road and down a steep ravine. In split seconds, she flipped down the embankment. About halfway to the bottom her helmet struck a huge oak tree with tremendous force.

The truck driver jumped out of their truck and shrieked to the 911 operator, "I think I just hit a lady who is lying at the bottom of a ravine. She looks dead! What do I do?"

Once she was medically examined, the doctors determined Coach Cato's coma was caused by the blunt-force trauma from her head striking the large oak. She also sustained several minor abrasions and substantial bruising, though no other serious internal injuries.

The news of Coach Cato's horrific accident spread all over school the next day. During her lunch break, Anne convinced her father to take her to visit her coach in the hospital. Lying about being family, Anne took her first dreadful step into the hospital room. She couldn't believe her eyes. Her coach had nasty cuts and bruises all over her once perfect complexion. Her athletic body lay motionless with tubes and wires traveling everywhere. She looked far more dead than alive.

Anne mustered up the courage to step closer. "Hey, Coach," Anne whispered, not knowing how to talk to a person who she figured wasn't really there. "You are going to survive this. I know it. You are a fighter." She waited to see if her words had any magical effect. "Now I am telling you like you tell us, 'No matter what the score, never, never give up.' And Coach, you better fight like never before because you are a boatload of points behind right now."

Anne helplessly sunk down into the chair next to the bed. She looked through her tears at her only idol in her life, lying totally lifeless. The only evidence of life was the vacillating numbers on the monitors connected to her body. Anne sat there, not knowing what to think or say. "Is anyone even home?" she dared to question. The queen felt as helpless as her coach looked.

Without warning, Anne's hopelessness turned into anger. "You failed me! I trusted you, but you failed me. When you needed a win, how many times did I come through for you? Look at you now. You and your big mouth about consequences and stuff...and look who fell off the cliff!"

Anne quickly left when family members started arriving. Sitting in her father's car while heading back to school, Anne's dad inquired about Coach Cato and the accident. "So, did Coach Cato have her helmet on?"

"Yeah. She always wore a helmet."

"Was she on the right side of the road?"

"She always rides on the dirt shoulder to avoid cars."

"Was she wearing brightly colored clothes?"

Exasperated from the visit and all her father's questions, Anne curtly replied, "Dad, Coach obeyed all the laws. She never deserved this. Some butthead truck driver needs to rot in prison for three lifetimes."

Every day after school Anne's father took her to visit her coach. She held many one-way conversations. Sometimes the trivial stuff of the day, other times she reviewed what Coach Cato previously taught her on their trips to volleyball games.

Finally, on the fourth day, about to burst from her pent-up bitter feelings of loss, Anne attacked. "Coach, how could you let this happen? You lost everything and you screwed up my life in the process. You talked so smart, but look at you now. You got less brains than a cantaloupe."

Anne paused and cried, "I just wish you could help me. Coach, I'm lost. I feel like nothing is promised to us. Nothing. Why work hard if an idiot can destroy everything? Why do what is right if you end up dead, if not for the machines?"

Anne sank her head into her coach's chest, sobbing, "Come back to me! I need you. You are my grip on life. If you don't make it, I know I don't stand a chance."

After a few minutes, Anne regained her composure and starting pacing the floor at the foot of Coach Cato's bed. She thought out loud about the meaning of her life.

"What does everything boil down to? This is reality. I lost my relationship with Coach, now everything seems so shallow and empty. Nothing else matters much."

Looking at the clock, she realized others would soon be coming to visit. She ducked out and met her dad as he returned from running errands. "I need to come back tomorrow," she flatly requested of her father. "Unfinished business," was all she was willing to add.

Again, after school the following day, Anne's dad took her to the hospital while he worked on his computer in the waiting room. Anne snuck by the nurses' desk in her typical fashion and went straight to her coach's room.

"Well, Coach, another day in paradise I see. Me too, except for failing my chemistry test, not showing up for volleyball practice, being late to two worthless classes, and getting into a slight bit of trouble for sweetly telling my English teacher where she could stick Shakespeare. Personally, I thought it was a clever pun, but I guess the admin folks want me to take three days off from school to keep you company."

Anne took a deep breath and returned to reality, "Well, what's the use. Good people get what bad people deserve. Why not live self-consumed? At least the queen lives large until hell hits."

Anne sat down and became honest with herself. "I hate what I am looking at. Coach, you are my rock and you just got smashed into pieces. I am not going to run and hide from this. Anne has no fear."

Instantly, the word "fear" reminded Anne of her last conversation with Coach. "Coach was saying I had fear of losing my control on life and that demanding control was destroying relationships in my life."

Anne walked into the adjacent bathroom to wash the tears from her face. While drying her face she overheard a man's voice. "Honey, I missed you terribly last night. I can't enjoy dinner without you. I miss hearing your voice, seeing your smile, and hearing about your day. I miss knowing about the game or how your talks with Anne went."

"Honey," his voice cracked, "I adore you and you know I would trade places with you if I could, but then you would suffer instead of me. Please come back to me. But, if you don't, I am thankful for being able to love you as you were and even as you are now. This way I suffer instead of you."

Anne heard a short pause, then she deciphered between moans, "Loving you gives me reason to breathe. I am not sure I can keep breathing without you. If I can't love you, I am ruined."

Anne listened as the man sobbed uncontrollably. She peered out the crack in the door to see him lying on the bed alongside his wife, with his head buried in her pillow next to her head. Quietly, Anne snuck out of the room and into the hallway. Shaken up over his incredible love for his wife, Anne took the stairs down to hide her tears from others.

Crawling onto the backseat of her father's car, she curled up into a ball without a word.

Suspended from school the following day, Anne's thoughts tormented her as she remembered Mr. Cato's words, "Loving you gives me reason to breathe. If I can't love you, I am ruined." It sounded so painfully rich. But is love really worth the risk?

On his way to the office, Anne's father asked her if she wanted to visit her coach. Anne simply answered, "I gotta get some answers," as she grabbed her coat.

Entering the room, Anne had flashbacks of Mr. Cato's pain, as if he still lay next to her. Checking the bathroom first to make sure she was alone, she looked at her coach and pondered, "Your husband practically crumbled into pieces. He really loves you for you, not himself. What would sharing a love like that be like? It must be fantastic because he doesn't want to live life without it. But how do you survive when you lose your loved one? How can two people who love each other not fear the inevitable death-breaker?"

"Again, I say 'fear.' You were right, Coach. Fear actually controls me because it will never allow me to love someone like your husband loves you. I want to control others to serve me."

Anne paced the floor as a second question came to her, "So, is it better to once share the joy of love and suffer the bitter pain when it is gone, than not share love at all?" She considered her own life. "Well, not much chance of me ever finding out. Like you said, Coach, 'I am consumed with pleasing Queen Anne.' I know I am loved, but I am about as lovable as a tumbleweed."

Anne walked to the head of Coach Cato's bed and spoke softly, "Actually, I have been rethinking my earlier comments to you, about you putting your foot in your mouth about who was going to fall over the cliff. You never promised me you would live long, but that you knew best how to live. And, what is the point of living a hundred years if you never experience a relationship like you share with your honey?"

Pacing back and forth, Anne continued, "Your broken-in-a-thousand-pieces husband was a little bit of evidence that got me rethinking things. You completely gave yourselves to each other. You knew how to give and that changes people." Anne asked herself, "Who has Queen Anne ever given anything to? I abuse people. My dad, my boyfriends, my teammates. I'm just a taker."

Anne leaned over only inches from her Coach's swollen face, "I want to be loved like you are loved—deservingly. I want someone to come and drench my pillow with tears and snot like your husband does for you, even if I never know it. I want someone who will love me enough to wish they outlive me because they would rather suffer the pain instead of me. Even in a coma, what you have easily outranks my being queen of my life."

Walking back to the parking lot, Anne repeatedly asked herself, "Will I ever love someone more than I love my own queendom? Or, will my fear of letting go of my crown turn me into a lonely witch?"

What Love is Worth

Every drinker knows that waking up in the morning with a throbbing hangover is the price you pay for drinking too much the night before. Likewise, fear, stress, anger, and hopelessness are the hangovers of living to serve one's own kingdom. Serving God's kingdom "the night before" will reward you with peace, joy, and contentment. There is a sequence and we reap what we sow, upper hell or lower heaven.

"Whatever a man sows, that he will also reap" (Galatians 6:7).

Every anxious person knows they didn't reap anxiety by simply demanding it. "I insist on being fearful this minute." Anxiety is caused by our first worshiping our stuff. We fear it getting destroyed. Nor does it help to say, "I really need peace this moment," after hearing the doctor's bad news. Peace comes when first recognizing God is in control and our stuff and bodies are not our own.

The necessary sequence exists because there is an inescapable cause and effect relationship between 1) our choice of who we choose to serve, and 2) the outcome our choice produces. If we first hand over our domains to Jesus before they get smashed, then we will still enjoy His peace even when they do. Conversely, if we pursue building our domains, then we will suffer continual anxiety. "I have learned both to be full and to be hungry, both to abound and to suffer need. I can do all things through Christ who strengthens me" (Philippians 4:12-13).

Are you wondering how much of our hearts God wants us to love Him back with? "You shall love the Lord your God with all your heart, with all your soul, and with all your strength" (Deuteronomy 6:5). All. Not "most" of your heart, soul, and strength.

"All" is a very big, little word. It's a "hard to satisfy" expectation. Anything less than "all" would be unloving, leaving us sampling the bondage of upper hell. As we choose to love Him over our lives, He will transform our hearts with His selflessness. *The more we love with God's quality of selfless love, the more we become "fit containers" for Him to fill us with everything that makes life worth living.*

God is still easy to please in our growing in "all."

To some, "all" looks like an endless treacherous mountain to climb. But God rewards each step forward. He loves it when we surrender that one angry thought we loved to brew about. He loves it when we quit insisting that He explain Himself for what happened years ago. He loves it when we stop critically judging others, one person at a time. *He loves it when we finally realize that trusting Him "mentally blindfolded" isn't really covering up much.*

God blesses and spends His kid's domains as He deems. Our obedience to love Him may bring huge rewards here and now. Or, it may cost us our lives, just as God required His

Son's life to accomplish His plan. "He who did not spare His own Son, but delivered Him up for us all" (Romans 8:32).

If our hearts have truly turned from selfish to selfless, then our strength is transferred away from serving our domains to instead bringing joy to the heart of God. *Our mantra becomes, "Whatever brings joy to the heart of God—that is what I have the strength for."* Not just, *"The joy of the Lord is your strength" (Nehemiah 8:10).*

8

God's Trash Talk

Opening Thoughts

Rational people say, "If it can't be reasonably explained, it probably isn't worth much. Definitely not worth committing one's life to." There are countless rational people who keep God at a distance, claiming, "I just can't get my mind wrapped around Him."

Others believe their spiritual relationship with God is restricted to the truths they read in His Word. Black ink on white paper is where they put their boundaries on who God is and how He wants to speak to them.

How inconsistent. *The very things that affect us the greatest in life can't be put into words. Everyone knows that it's life's most powerful experiences that leave us speechless. No word or any combination of words in the entire dictionary, in any language, can adequately express our soul's encounter with things of true power.*

Words do no justice to effectively describe life's most powerful moments, such as:

- The first gaze into the open eyes of a newborn that just came out of your own womb.
- When one's world is caving in and they find it hard to breathe.
- When a man recklessly abandons his life out of love for his wife and family.
- The devastated soul of a parent after losing their child.
- The proud heart of a father when his uniformed son steps off the plane, returning safely from war.
- When music captures the distraught soul and takes it to an unknown place of peace and comfort.
- When a soul is captivated by a fiery sunset, magnificently mirrored over an endless ocean.

The moments that define us, moments of true power, are those that can't be put into words without severely diminishing the essence of the experience.

Since our life-changing experiences in our natural world, which we readily recognize as the most powerful, remain inexpressible, how much more should we find God's supernatural world beyond our finite vocabulary? Do we really want God's essence to be so simple that we could wrap our minds around Him? He would become more boring than a puppy within an hour.

Being at a loss for words to explain God's love and how He works reminds us of our smallness. It's the same overwhelmed feeling one gets when trying to stare down the sun. Paul reminds us in Ephesians 3:19-20, "To know the love of Christ which passes knowledge; that you may be filled with all the fullness of God. Now to Him who is able to do exceedingly abundantly above all that we ask or think, according to the power that works in us" (see also Psalm 139:1-16; Romans 8:26-27; and Ephesians 1:8).

That being said, imagine how God must feel when trying to communicate His incredible truths using our words? Perhaps like rummaging through a dumpster to put together a gourmet meal? If we don't have the vocabulary to do justice to describing anything of true power in the natural, do you really think black ink on white paper does God's supernatural love any justice?

Anne's Story: Part Four

It was later in the evening and after regular visiting hours, but Anne desperately wanted to visit her coach. She approached her father and bargained, "Dad, if you take me to see Coach, I will buy you ice cream on the way home." He agreed, always looking for opportunities to spend time with his daughter. Springing out of the car just past the ambulance parking curb, Anne wasted no time as she snuck past the nurses' station and slipped into Coach Cato's room.

She studied the room full of flowers and cards from her Coach's family and friends. Then she noticed the volleyball at the foot of the bed. Picking it up, she realized the entire team had signed it—everyone, but her. "Wow," she spoke out loud. "What a face-plant."

Anne knew this was not just "another day in paradise" for her. Her heart was swollen with emotion and on the verge of making life-changing decisions. She realized how little control she really had on life. How small she was. She needed answers.

"Some mentor you turned out to be. Just when I am ready to listen to your advice, you have nothing to say. Well, I figured out a few things over the last couple of days. Mostly that my selfish existence isn't worth it. I want someone to come and drench my pillow with tears and snot if I go full cantaloupe head. Someone who really loves me even if I can give nothing back, because I already loved them selflessly."

Anne continued, "And frankly, now, for me, pre-cantaloupe head is no good either. All my hugs and kisses come from myself. My self-absorbed life has no meaning when I am all alone and realize no one really cares. The MVP can't even get her name on a team volleyball." Anne grinned, "Coach, you will be glad to know that I am sticking the queen in the dungeon, somewhere she isn't the boss of me."

After confessing those words, Anne collapsed back into her chair. A wave of anguish swept over her as she realized the great tragedy that had to happen to get her to speak those words. Anne started to cry, "I am sorry it took this…" She clutched her stomach, her indescribable pain dropping her to the floor. She lay there several moments, crumbled up and moaning deeply. Finally, regaining her strength, she kneeled on the chair and spoke facing the chair's backrest, "I am dying the way I am living. To get me to own up to my selfishness almost cost my coach her life. And I'm sure that if my coach had known what it would cost her, she would still say, 'It is worth it.' I am not going to waste Coach's life. Things are going to change."

Unknown to Anne, Mr. Cato was standing directly behind her, listening to her confession. Sensing someone in the room, Anne slowly turned around and recognized him through her tears. She realized, like herself, he had come late just to get some time alone with his wife. They simply stared at each other, sharing the other's loss. For five minutes, tears streamed down both their cheeks and to the floor. Not a word was spoken.

Finally, Mr. Cato stepped closer, kissed the delicate white and purple orchid he had come in with, and placed it into Anne's open palms. Staring kindly into her eyes, he briefly smiled and left.

All Anne could think of was how unworthy she was to receive such a precious gift meant for her coach. Then, studying the orchid, she realized it was picked because it was beautiful. It symbolized her coach. It struck Anne, "Mr. Cato gave me who Coach is. He just assigned to me her true beauty. I think I just got my new start."

Anne cherished the orchid, but not ready to explain it to her father, she hid it in her coat. On their way home, Anne kept her promise and treated her father to ice cream. As they ate their ice cream together, she asked, "Dad, can I do a do-over?"

"What do you mean?"

"Well, I would like to start from scratch with you. No yesterdays. I want no bad history that can't be broken."

"I am good with that," her dad said.

"And, I know this sounds distrusting from the beginning, but I really only want to make this a three-month experiment. I am getting rid of Queen Anne. Sticking the witch in the dungeon, you might say."

Anne's dad laughed so hard the top scoop fell off his ice cream cone. "Ok, honey," he finally answered, "but during the three months you need to be all in. Really trying to get past what the queen taught you all your life."

"Yeah, well, I will probably move in very small steps. I hope you are still easy to please."

"Of course. And I have a present for you." Anne's dad reached into his pocket and pulled out a well-worn box. "This is for you," he smiled.

Taken by surprise, Anne opened it with a curious grin. Inside she found a pendant in the shape of a heart that read, "Always Open."

"Well, you knocked," beamed Anne's dad. "For three months, open is what we both agree to."

Anne's heart felt as though something new snuck in.

Beyond Words

It's the powerful moments in our lives that often leave us sobbing, exuberant, screaming, falling, covering our faces, awestruck, curled up in a fetal position, paralyzed, and almost always wordless. How much more must our dictionary horribly fail God when trying to explain His powerful truths? How inadequate are our finite words in describing His infinite wisdom? "Cheapened" doesn't even begin to describe what is lost in translation. "For we know in part" (First Corinthians 13:9).

God's written word is true and essential and must be continuously studied to grow in the fundamental nature of God. "All Scripture is given by inspiration of God, and is profitable for doctrine" (Second Timothy 3:16). However, there is a critical reason the Bible is the only book that comes with the Author. God's Spirit transforms the power of His written word, using His heart-to-heart communication. A powerful realization sneaks into the person with an open heart.

To one person, they read ordinary words. To another reading the exact same words, but with the Spirit's assistance, something registers far deeper in the soul, far beyond being capable of putting into words. Hebrews 4:12, "For the word of God is living and powerful, and sharper than any two-edged sword…and is a discerner of the thoughts and intents of the heart" (see also Isaiah 11:2, 59:2; Luke 12:12; John 3:34, 6:63, 14:14-17, and 16:7-14).

It is through this type of wordless communication that God gives us perfect peace in the midst of a storm, courage when all is hopeless, love for the unlovable, direction through chaos, wisdom when hitting an impossible impasse, and joy when all seems lost. "You search the Scriptures, for in them you think you have eternal life; and these are they which testify of Me. But you are not willing to come to Me that you may have life" (John 5:39-40).

It is through this type of wordless communication that God can change the course of one's entire life. It leaves a mark that can't be explained or removed. Something sneaks in. As with our natural experiences of power, moments of spiritual power remain beyond our ability to explain.

God's wordless revelation of Himself is never contrary to His written Word. It will always submit to it if God is the one doing the revealing. As Paul reminded his protégé, Timothy, in Second Timothy 1:13, "Hold fast the pattern of sound words," and in 2:15, "Be diligent to present yourself approved to God" (see also First Corinthians 2:14; Ephesians 6:17; and First Thessalonians 1:5-6).

9

Flavor Freedom

Opening Thoughts

Not all obedience is created equal. One child goes through the motions of obedience to avoid punishment. But they hate submitting. Another child obeys only for the promised reward. No reward, no obedience.

Then, there is the child who desires to please their parents. Although they confidently know how generously their parents desire to reward them, they obey out of love for their parents, not for self-centered reasons. Only this kind of obedience is what God is after because it starts with "right being" before ending in "right doing" (Hebrews 11:6).

Living moral but without the selfless heart of God is like the child that obeys, but only for selfish reasons. Their motivation remains purely selfish, thinking they can manipulate God into supporting their "it's all about me" attitude. To God, that kind of obedience looks no different than living immoral and against Him. "You are those who justify yourselves before men, but God knows your hearts. For what is highly esteemed among men is an abomination in the sight of God" (Luke 16:15).

Selfishness often proudly dresses up in morality to get what it wants.

To obey with the right motives requires an infusion of God's selfless heart. The problem is source availability. To operate selflessly, one must receive the pure nature of God through the indwelling of His Spirit. "I am the vine, you are the branches...without Me you can do nothing" (John 15:5).

Look at this truth from God's fathering angle. God went through the enormous expense of giving the life of His Son to enable us to walk in harmony with His selfless (holy) nature. "Can two walk together, unless they are agreed?" (Amos 3:3). Jesus died to walk in oneness with us—a true friendship. How much joy would Jesus receive if all He got in return for His enormous sacrifice were "friends" whose driving motivation for every little act of obedience was only a "candy bar" payoff? Or those who obey only to avoid a spanking? Some friendship.

Our underlying motives determine the quality of our love produced. When selfless love doesn't drive our obedience, we are simply exchanging outward rebellion for inward indifference. Frauds. We act kind to someone while despising them. Yet, Christ loves us and died so we can love Him and others with His pure quality of love. His heart breaks because He wants to bless us, but our selfish quality of love disallows it (John 17:23; Romans 5:5; Second Corinthians 5:17).

After becoming true to Christ's heart, we can pick and choose to walk in a thousand different directions, and in each we represent Him. Starting with His nature within us, God grants us the freedom to make countless personal choices of our liking. *We enjoy the best of both worlds, His and ours.*

Anne's Story: Part Five

On the way home from the ice cream parlor, Anne anticipated how she was going to keep her commitment to her father the next morning. She decided to press her father for what to expect.

"So, I throw the queen in the dungeon, but how do we do things? I mean…do I need to ask you about every little thing?"

"Not at all. In fact, I want you to enjoy your passions," explained her dad.

"Well, I am in new territory here. Plus, we really don't have any real history of working together."

Her dad smiled. "Then think of your new territory as a wide area for you to be yourself in, but it has an outside fence, or guardrails. Boundaries that can be referred to as what is 'loving' and 'right.'" Anne's father continued, "Tonight, for example. The ice cream parlor offers many flavors for you to choose from. I want you to pick your favorites, but being loving and right keeps you from crossing boundaries such as stealing, being rude, eating too much, or, if you were diabetic, eating a bunch of sugar."

"So I have 'flavor freedom' to pick Rocky Road or Mint Chip. And you set the boundaries for my own benefit," Anne nodded, remembering her coach telling her about the rules of volleyball.

Anne's dad elaborated, "Loving and right summarize the way your coach lived: honest, fair, truthful, selfless, and encouraging. Everything you love about her. So, you will have to trust me that the boundaries I set as loving and right are best for you. However, your queen won't like it."

"Really?" Anne seemed a little surprised. "I don't see how the queen cares that much?"

"She will go on scream mode when I ask you to do something against serving yourself. Like being nice to someone that was rude to you. But you must realize they are hurting too and they need someone to help them through a hard time. So, you spend yourself a little."

"Yeah, I can see how that changes things for the queen, but that is what Coach Cato did for me. I get it. It may be a blood bath, but the queen must lose for three months. That's the deal."

Her dad continued, "I have no problem with how many rounds you go with the queen, I only care about me winning in the end. I know you've got history with her. She screams and fights dirty. It will take some time to shake her annoying voice and convincing arguments."

Anne appreciated her father's understanding attitude. "I was a bit concerned that you would be upset if you knew how much I might be leaning toward listening to the queen when it comes to your really high expectations."

"It doesn't upset me that she scores a few hard punches. What matters to me is that you choose my way in the end. And, for you to get a better idea of the boundaries part, we will need to spend time talking. Like breakfast at the café once a week."

"So," Anne reflected, a little hesitant, "you are going to lay down the rules on how I dress, what boyfriend I choose, and when I go to bed?"

"Hang on, Anne. I don't want you to get the idea that you are now enslaved to rules. This needs to be about your heart being open to pleasing my heart. Freely. Because you want to, not because you have to."

Anne's dad grew very serious. "You said no yesterdays. Well, all your yesterdays were driven by your need to control to get what you wanted. Now, your todays need to be driven by your decision to operate within right and loving, and you still enjoy your flavor freedom."

Anne thought quietly, *Well, I have freedom to be myself, but not serve myself. Not sure how that figures out, but the queen loses her throne and that freaks her out. On the other hand, if the queen reigns, I live and die alone because she rules like the Wicked Witch of the West. How painful can it be to live with guardrails? Coach loved it.*

"Ok, Dad," Anne ended like she was closing a business deal. "My buy-in looks like this. For three months I am totally in. The queen shuts her pie-hole. I learn and agree with your heart's boundaries and my focus is on making you proud of me."

Anne's dad smiled. "Just know that I love you and this really isn't about me."

Living Free

When we live within the nature of the heart of God, He gives us freedom to make personal choices that excite our hearts. For example, if a single person is looking for a spouse, God's heart says, "Pick anyone you like, but remember My boundaries. Choose someone who wants to serve Me. They will take on the family likeness: giving and forgiving, placing others first, and being humble, teachable, and kind to those who can't pay them back."

By staying within His guardrails, God gives us the freedom to pick the kind of person we desire. It's no different than buying a house or car, choosing a career, or choosing what to wear. "Is it building my domain or God's kingdom?" "Does it make me feel like I am better than others?" "Can I afford it?" "Am I drawing attention to myself?" Ask Him if it honors Him and if so, buy what you like.

Of course, there are times when God's boundaries are not clear. Such as, "God, what do You think about me buying these state-of-the-art speakers? They are half-price!" The money is not breaking your budget and the high-end speakers are something that you would really like, but you also know the new speakers are not really necessary.

If, after praying nothing comes to your mind for or against the purchase, then ask, "God, do You give me permission to buy these speakers?" Wait for the response, "Sure, enjoy yourself," or "No, let them go."

Does getting permission sound like God's way of fathering? Or perhaps a little too much freedom for self-gratification? Maybe, but look at the extravagance God used in creating us: giving us our amazing taste buds, incredible color vision, various fragrant aromas, and sex! Obviously, God wants us to enjoy our lives within His guidance (John 2:1-11).

Is God upset that we wrestle to love Him over other loves? Is He insulted that He actually competes with our love over frivolous idols like ice cream, entertainment, and sports? Or our offensive idols like gossip, lust, and vain imaginations? God knows our hearts are a mixed bag of affections.

The harder the contest, the greater the love required to choose one over the other. God is not shocked about our love for the absurd. In the end, the one you choose is the one you love, even if you sweat bullets making the decision to obey. "Nevertheless, not as I will, but as You will" (Matthew 26:39).

10

Following Instructions

Opening Thoughts

God leads us in two primary ways. First, through learning and obeying His selfless nature, He flows through us. When God sees His kindness flow through us, it delights Him and others see Him in us.

Then secondly, by listening to His Spirit's leading. His Spirit may interrupt our lives and place a specific "mission" for us individually. "God, is there anything You want me to do for that family?" He may direct your mind to think about helping them with transportation or maintaining their house.

Through the first way we take on Christ's nature—we become forgiving, generous, honest, etc. Through the second manner, we hear from Him via a distinctive nudge on the heart. "Help those people over there with their problem." Obeying God on both of these lines may be referred to as "walking in the will of God."

Unfortunately, our selfish birth nature is very mischievous and deceives us easier than a ventriloquist at a nursey school party. *When changing our behavior, we naively believe that because we stopped lying and started telling the truth, that God is the one making the improvement.* We don't question if our selfish nature simply determined, "I am a terrible liar and it gets me into trouble?" We actually tell the truth when it serves us, which is why we feel comfortable lying at other occasions. "Just tell them we can't make it."

Additionally, regarding obeying the Spirit's voice, instead of praying to listen to God's specific directions, we naively tune into our selfish nature's opinion that puts words into God's mouth. Instead of asking God, "Do these mean thoughts offend You?" We say to ourselves, "God understands my harboring these mean thoughts…"

To combat our deceptive nature that effortlessly cons us, we must honestly invite God's Spirit to challenge our hearts. "What do You see as the attitudes of my heart? Do I hold onto unforgiveness?" Only the Holy Spirit will expose the dark areas of our hearts that our sin nature swears doesn't exist. Consequently, the closer one gets to the Light, the more imperfections they will find in themselves (John 3:19-20, 12:36-40).

Expect to wrestle with God as He exposes our hidden motives. Beware of wrestling against Him. We should want what He wants. *Our goal, in time, is to pray and listen to His Spirit with no heart of our own in the matter. In time, our hearts become molded into His. His nature and direction become our first nature.*

Anne's Story: Part Six

At least once a week Anne and her father enjoyed breakfast together at the local country café. Anne loved her blueberry waffles and slowly grew to enjoy her dad's company. As he spoke about life, she grew in her understanding of his heart. After a few weeks, Anne's father thought it was the right time to give her an opportunity to test her "flavor freedom" in obeying his parenting.

After school on Friday, Anne's dad explained, "I would like to give you some money to do whatever you want this weekend. If you need a ride, let me know." With that he gave her a generous amount of cash.

Anne looked at the money and "shopping" instantly popped into her head. Then, she caught herself and thought, *What can I do to please my dad, but something that would also fit for me?* Her mind immediately shot to spending time with her coach, but also making it special.

That night, Anne downloaded a couple of movies on her tablet, then got pizza before her dad dropped her off at the hospital after visiting hours. Her parting instructions to her father were, "I'll call you if they kick me out before morning...and thanks."

As Anne entered her coach's room, she joked, "Thought you might like a change of menu. And, unless you strongly object, you and I are going to hang out together tonight." Anne waved her tablet in front of her comatose coach. "I picked out a movie with you in mind...so do your best to act like it is the first time you have ever seen it."

As the night rolled on, Anne realized how enjoyable it was to think of others first. "Well, Coach, I wish you could know, if only in your heart, that I chose being with you tonight because I care about you. You are the only one that means this much to me. And, I have been doing something else. I eat breakfast now with my dad. You were right. He is on my side." Anne added, "In case you were wondering where 'my hotness' went, I stuck the queen in the dungeon for three months."

The following morning, the nurses all laughed as they directed Anne's dad to her coach's room. They found Anne sound asleep, curled up next to her coach with an empty pizza box, except for the pizza crusts, which were scattered like bones on top of her coach's stomach.

"Time to go, honey," he said as he gently nudged her shoulder. "Coach Cato's family will come soon and the nurses need to do their thing."

On their way out, Anne noticed a new lady in the room next to her coach. "Did she arrive in the middle of the night?" Anne asked the night nurse.

"Yes. Another auto accident. Just her though...she probably fell asleep at the wheel."

"Will she be ok?"

"It looks good for her. Hopefully, only a few broken ribs, but more tests will tell."

Anne peeked her head inside the new arrival's hospital room. "Hey Dad, can I just say something to this poor lady? She looks all alone."

"Sure."

Anne casually walked into her room like she owned the hospital. "Hi, I'm Anne. Anything I can do for you?"

The lady smiled, medicated, but still in pain. "Actually, yes. It's asking a lot, but I have two dogs that will need food and water until I get out of here. I live alone. Could you do that for me?"

Anne looked at her dad for his consent. He nodded. Anne replied, "Consider it done. Tell my dad where you live and I will feed your dogs. What are their names?"

"Cuff and Link."

"Really? Like the turtles in the Rocky movie?"

"Yeah. Not real original, but the names fit."

The woman started to give directions to her house when Anne realized it was close to her coach's house. "Wow, I know that road. Close to your house a man just ran my coach off the road and almost killed her. She is in a coma in the next room. I just spent the night…"

"When did she get hit?" interrupted the lady.

"Just over three weeks ago."

The lady closed her eyes and turned her head. Anne looked at her father, not knowing if she had said something wrong.

"Did you see the ambulance?" Anne asked.

"I called the ambulance."

"I was told the butthead truck driver called the ambulance."

"She did."

Anne again glanced at her father, hoping she misunderstood. "Are you saying you smashed my coach into the oak tree and down the cliff?"

"I swerved to miss my neighbor's runaway dog. With the sun's glare...I never saw your coach until it was too late. I haven't slept over three hours a night since."

Anne stepped back with shock in her eyes. How could she show mercy to the driver she wanted to rot in prison for three lifetimes?

Anne's dad spoke up, "It was a terrible accident, but still an accident. And I trust you will recover quickly from your injuries. Anne will take care of your dogs until you can get better. We need to get going."

On the way home, Anne finally broke the long silence. "Well, Dad, the queen is screaming, 'Hate her!' I mean, it's bloody murder in the dungeon. Why should I help someone who destroyed the life of the greatest coach in the world?"

"Well, if you feed her dogs, they will live and grow stronger. But if you starve them, they will get weaker until they die. For you, if you feed the anger you have in your heart toward this lady by holding on to it, you will continue to be tormented and it will grow stronger. But if you don't feed it, it will grow weaker and eventually die. Now, you tell me, would a loving father want his daughter to suffer in misery, or live in freedom?"

"But does that mean I have to do something nice for her? Why can't I find someone else to feed her dogs? I shouldn't have to be the one."

"Well, when you were mean to me, I did you right. You sometimes spoke very cruel to me, when I tried to be nice to you."

"Holy crap!" Anne yelled as she slapped her forehead. "This must be the hard to satisfy part. I don't know if you can hear, but the queen is screaming, 'Revenge, you idiot,' while tearing apart the entire dungeon." Driving up to the house, Anne asked cautiously, "The queen wants to make a deal. If I do this, Coach Cato gets better."

Anne's dad chuckled, "More than anything, the queen hates doing something for nothing in return, especially to someone who has hurt you." Anne's dad finished, "But there is nothing more exciting to a father than when his daughter obeys for no other reason than to please him."

Anne jumped out as her father pulled into Ms. Smyth's driveway. Opening the gate, two of the happiest dogs she had ever met came running and jumped all over her.

"Hi Cuff and Link. Or, Link and Cuff." Aren't you two boys the most adorable dogs in town?" Anne filled their bowls and water dish as they jumped on her legs. Getting back into her father's car, Anne slapped her stomach and growled, "Shut up down there, you crazy witch."

Anne's dad laughed so hard he started snorting. After composing himself, he sighed with tears in his eyes, "If you only knew how much you mean to me."

Our Freedom at God's Expense

Our primary problem with making godly decisions isn't that we struggle to know what pleases God. It's that the king or queen in us doesn't want to pay the cost. "Father, should I help my co-worker finish their work? They have never helped me." We want to remain selfish in our decisions. We get just enough of God in our lives, stopping at the point of really turning over control of our domains.

We might reason that a 97% obedience in one or two coveted areas of our lives should satisfy God. Areas like money, food, time, offenses, stuff, dreams, skills, families, etc. *Sadly, that itty bitty 3% we still control will turn into a convenient catch-all for anything that demands a selfless sacrifice that we don't want to obey. Holding onto a 97% mindset, we are really controlling God. In essence, we are dictating to Him where He is and isn't "King."*

Nothing makes our selfish nature scream bloody murder louder than returning kindness for evil. But to God, returning kindness for evil, His attribute of grace, ranks the most beautiful of all His attributes because it cost Him the most. It requires the purist selfless love behind it, like no other attribute requires. *When His children give grace, it hits the bullseye of the heart of God.* Returning kindness for evil proves our love back as selfless and represents Him to the fullest to a guilt-ridden world.

Why is grace the most beautiful attribute of God? Price.

Before sin entered the world, God could reveal to all mankind every attribute but one, grace. God allowed sin because He wanted everyone to fully witness the depth of His love for mankind, to the highest degree possible. In choosing to reveal this one attribute, grace, it cost Him the price of His Son and countless heartbreaks over mankind's disobedience. Sin was never a surprise to God that caused Him to switch to "Plan B." The cross was decided on before creation. Revealing His costly grace is the reason (First Peter 1:19-20; Revelation 13:8).

After God forgives us, He doesn't conveniently get rid of us. Nor does God forgive us to rid His mind of anger. He doesn't forgive us and then disown us for the bad memories of our terrible offenses. That would remain self-serving. In fact, He wants to bless us more. He forgives, then gives the gift of Himself. His forgiveness is for our benefit and our accepting it brings His life into our life.

If we refuse to offer the same forgiveness Christ offers us, we offend His gift of Himself to us. Our insult could not be greater. The severe consequences of our stingy grace fits our egregious offense. "But if you do not forgive men their trespasses, neither will your Father forgive your trespasses" (Matthew 6:15). Not giving grace begs the question if it was ever truly received to begin with (Matthew 18:21-35, 25:30, 46).

Do we truly understand God's forgiveness? Have we received it? If so, we will walk out what He has worked in. Only when walking in oneness with Christ will we live free of anger, fear, and self-pity. God designed us and wants us to live by His design. When we do, we will love our lives regardless of how deeply others have injured us.

"But love your enemies, do good, and lend, hoping for nothing in return; and your reward will be great, and you will be sons of the Most High. For He is kind to the unthankful and evil" (Luke 6:35).

11

Walking Out What God Has Worked In

Opening Thoughts

As stated, we walk in oneness with God by living out His character and secondly by following specific direction. His character flows through us as we yield to His selfless nature in us, not when we are kind for selfish reasons.

His direction comes to us through His Spirit, giving us "nudges" to do a specific work. He may nudge us by giving impressions. Impressions that honor Him. Sometimes the Spirit causes thoughts to just "dawn" on us through prayer. Other times He uses specific verses or other people who speak into our lives. Occasionally He gives us dreams.

His character never changes and it is never our option to disregard while following His specific instructions. God doesn't condone, "I believe God wants me to run for city council, but I need to mislead the voters when discrediting my opponent to make myself look good."

God also gives us the privilege of being ourselves while doing both. We can still enjoy our "flavor freedom" while living out His character. "Hey George, sorry about your car accident. If you want a ride, I feel like getting Thai food. Join me? My treat."

God also gives us flavor freedom as we yield to His specific instruction. "God keeps impressing me to encourage lonely folks who are staying in assisted living homes. I like crafts. I think that sounds like fun and I can put a little joy in their day."

With the freedom God gives, we exercise our passions and creativity within His guardrails. We ponder, "I wonder how much pleasure God gets when He sees us pour out His selfless love in our own ingenious ways?"

He loves to see us thrive in our strengths and passions, while we enjoy living "fueled" on His nature. Even so, the closeness of God's heart to our heart gets even more bewildering. (Colossians 1:16)

God, being a God of choice, gives us a third amazing option in our walking with Him. God has actually gifted us with a capability to amaze Him (Luke 7:1-10). We possess the ridiculous potential to do something that causes God's heart to marvel! We can impress the Creator of the universe with our going above and beyond what He has specifically told us to do. (Matthew 8:5-13, 15:21-28; John 2:4)

That should send chills down your spine.

Anne's Story: Part Seven

On their way home from feeding Cuff and Link, Anne's father stated, "I am impressed with your kindness toward your coach and for feeding Ms. Smyth's dogs. Imagine the pain Ms. Smyth must feel. It was a terrible accident, but still an accident. She hasn't slept for so long that she fell asleep while driving only a short distance."

"Stop dancing around and just tell me what you are getting at?" snapped Anne.

"Put Ms. Smyth on your list of people that you know need help."

"Really, Dad? That list is way too short to be called a list. And all 'busted ribs' has going for her is…well, her dogs are adorable."

"Just put her on your list and give it time. An idea will come. It may be a little strange, but you will know that it is no ordinary idea by the power it will have."

Getting out of the car, Anne went straight to her bedroom to catch up on some sleep. She pondered what her father meant by "a little strange." Crawling under her covers, Anne sighed. "Wow. I've already got ridiculously demanding stuff hitting me just three weeks in. The queen has nine weeks left on her sentence! I should have thought to make this a month-to-month kind of deal. Hopefully, she will lose her voice before long."

Anne fell into a deep sleep. Suddenly, an outlandish dream about her coach startled her out of her sleep. Waking up, she recalled dreaming that Coach Cato woke up from her coma, then walking into Ms. Smyth's room, and saying, "I release you."

The dream sent shivers down Anne's spine. That was just the kind of thing coach would break out of a coma to do. She would never want someone else to suffer on her account. Anne wasn't sure what the dream meant for her, but she knew the answer would come.

"Hey Dad, are you planning to go anywhere near the hospital today?"

"Again?" he asked incredulously, then added, "I made an appointment at Bob's garage to change the oil. I can drop you off on my way there."

That afternoon, Anne got her ride and made her way past her coach's busy room. Stopping by the nurses' station, Anne questioned, "Can you tell me Ms. Smyth's first name?"

"Sure." Looking at her chart, the nurse replied, "Cathy, spelled with a 'C'."

Walking through Cathy's doorway, Anne asked, "Hey Cathy with a 'C.' Is it ok to come in?"

"Sure. Did you find my house?"

"Oh yeah. Cuff and Link are adorable. But I am here for something else." With that, Anne pulled a slightly wilted purple and white orchid out of her coat and gently held it in front of Cathy.

After taking a deep breath, Anne explained, "This orchid was a gift to me that released me from my past. You have no idea how cruel I was. It was meant for Coach Cato and its beauty fits the way her heart is, but her husband handed it to me instead. Crazy as it sounds, you might say that when he passed the orchid from her to me, he really placed on me everything good about her. It was his way of saying that I can be just as kind as Coach." Anne paused in thought, "One day, I hope someone will give me an orchid, not because I am messed up and need it, but because it fits me."

As Anne finished speaking, she noticed Cathy's room didn't have any flowers. She felt embarrassed for Cathy, but knew her room would have been no different.

"Why are you telling me all this?" Cathy naturally questioned.

"Well, honestly, this is hard and I feel stupid. But, I guess my coach wants me to pass her kindness around. So, I am just going to say it. If coach could, I know she would say exactly these three words to you, 'I release you.'"

With that, Anne gently handed Cathy the delicate orchid and left. Cathy, too stunned to respond, kept her eyes riveted on the beautiful orchid and recounted the history and meaning the orchid held. Finally, Cathy incredulously stated to herself, "How does Anne know her coach would say, 'I release you'? It's a nice gesture, but no orchid has the power to forgive a 'butthead' truck driver for destroying someone's life."

Later that evening, long after visiting hours, Cathy painfully got up and shuffled her way into Coach Cato's room with the orchid in hand. As she entered, she choked as she looked at Coach's swollen face. She gradually worked up the courage to touch her lifeless hand and then asked, "So, Coach, I got your special flower. But can it really release me? Do you release me?"

As Cathy looked around the room at all the flowers, she realized again that she had ruined the life of a deeply loved person. Wanting to torture herself by holding onto the guilt, Cathy looked at the orchid and asked, "Well then, withered orchid, can you forgive me of my terrible guilt?" Again, she got the answer she expected.

Turning to leave the room, Cathy thoughtfully questioned, "Anne should hate me and want to make me suffer. Instead, she offers me freedom while she suffers the loss of her coach. Where does a bratty teenage kid get that kind of kindness?"

Turning her head, she looked back at Coach Cato and nodded, "Anne must have learned it from you. Somehow, you really did give her the words to release me."

As Cathy labored to turn the corner into her room, the night nurse came to her side and helped her get back into bed, saying, "Honey, you have no business walking around." Seeing the wilted orchid and knowing Cathy had no flowers, the nurse suspected Cathy of stealing it from Mrs. Cato's room. She thought, *Obviously, Mrs. Cato won't miss it. No harm done.*

"Do you want me to put your orchid in some water?" the nurse asked. "We keep some leftover vases at the nurses' station."

At the risk of sounding over-medicated, Cathy asked the nurse, "Do you see any special power in this flower? Can it carry forgiveness?"

"If it came from a heart that possesses forgiveness, yes, I think so."

Cathy paused, then asked, "Do you think it can come from more than one heart? I mean, can forgiveness be given twice?"

"Perhaps the forgiveness gets even better with each person that receives it and then passes it on," said the nurse.

"Then this orchid needs your prettiest vase."

Summary

Anne obeyed the specific desire of her father to put Cathy on her list. Then, through a dream that registered clearly to Anne's heart what she needed to say, she used her flavor freedom to walk out what pleased her father. Strange but powerful. Three minutes and three words of power can change a life.

God uses many ways to communicate His specific directions. He may also use circumstances, visions, or an experience. Often, He uses meditating on His written Word. God may bring back an old memory, speak through a friend or stranger, and He often uses His creation (Psalm 119:15; Matthew 7:21-23; First Corinthians 1:27-28, 13:2; Second Peter 2:16).

Some find it helpful to ask God to "finger" His leading from a list of possibilities. Such as asking God, "Who do You want me to put on Your needs list today? Harry, Luke, Seth, Sam, TJ, Buddy…?" and then God often stops you at a particular person's name. "Buddy."

Then pray, "God, how do You want me to help Buddy…give him a gift, call him, help him fix something, take him out to lunch, confront him, teach him about a lesson I learned…?" Again, God often puts His finger on what He wants (Acts 15:28).

We can also ask God to tell us something we are avoiding or to tell us something we really do not want to hear. Then go down the "grocery list" of options for Him to choose from. "God, who do I have a wrong attitude toward? My spouse, my pastor, my neighbor, my boss, my co-worker, my parents…?" You will be surprised at how clearly God will answer you, provided that you really want to know.

God is looking for children who are not afraid to surrender their domains. As we obey His heart and leading, we can actually impress Him by creatively investing ourselves in loving Him back. No big splash required, just simply thinking and meditating on ways to bring a thrill to the heart of our Friend that we walk with.

12

Are You Free?

Opening Thoughts

Believing that a crisis causes anxiety is way off the mark. *Crises don't cause anxiety—crowns do.*

A torrential rain storm frightens everyone in a house built on sand. Inside the house built on a rock, the people sleep peacefully.

Storms reveal our prior decision of exactly who we elected to wear the "crown" in a particular area of our life. If we confidently decide to keep our crown when things are going smoothly, we also simultaneously confidently decide to manage our domain during a storm. However, if we decide to surrender our crown to God when things are good, we also naturally make Him responsible to carry us through the storm. *Whoever wears the crown assumes the responsibility.* "Casting all your care upon Him, for He cares for you" (First Peter 5:7).

Why don't we realize that clutching onto our crowns only causes anxiety and just get rid of them? Answer: Selfish living requires control. Crowns equal control. To someone who arrogantly wears their crown before the storm, their arrogance tries to "white knuckle" it when the storm hits.

Arrogance insists on keeping our crowns at all costs. We turn to options to reduce the stress that our crowns bring. "If all else fails, I can drink (or escape through a movie, book, work, exercise, trust medicine or psyche meds, shopping, hobby, sleeping, eating, and self-medicating)."

The crisis proves we fooled ourselves into thinking we were in control before it hit. Our anxiety is our proof we know we are not. Nothing like a pandemic to prove how much fear rules the world. So little rock, so much sand.

Crown-free is stress-free. When Christ wears the crown before the storm hits, our personal domains are no longer ours to fret over in the storm. Our "stuff" is no longer ours to control. We have decided to trust in His nature, not our need to remove the storm. Christ-ruled believers enjoy the freedom to dance through the storm. "My peace I give to you; not as the world gives" (John 14:27).

And when Jesus wears the crown, we rely on His love within us, not ours. "Me in me, not going to happen. Christ in me, now I can love anyone."

Anne's Story: Part Eight

Unlike Anne, Cathy's childhood felt like an inescapable eighteen-year nightmare. Her "queendom" looked more like a ghetto. As a young girl, Cathy was often verbally abused and physically slapped around by her wealthy stepfather.

Her vain mother conveniently turned a blind eye as she spent her husband's money to make herself look more glamorous. She routinely underwent cosmetic surgery to compete with younger women for her husband's devotion.

To excuse her stepfather's raging, Cathy's mother often made offhanded comments like, "Daddy sure does buy us nice things." To Cathy, her mother's words really meant, "Dad's money means I get to live large, which means more to me than his screaming at you. And him adoring my artificially enhanced body means more to me than him slapping yours."

Cathy knew she couldn't change her parents' self-absorbed lives. So, to give herself a sense of power, she focused on areas of her life that were under her control. As a young child, she enjoyed escaping to a pretend world with her dolls. At age ten, she tried not eating. In middle school, she went crazy cleaning and organizing her room. Throughout high school, she engrossed herself with wild hairstyles, boy's clothes, and music. But the little voice in her head never stopped whispering, *You don't matter*.

Currently, at the age of twenty-four, Cathy had long since moved out of her parents' home and was near finishing up her nursing program. She realized the "you don't matter" voice changed to "I think you are wonderful" when caring for hurting people in the hospital. Greater still, hurting folks were not likely to judge her. They were just thankful for being helped. No more cruel comments, just validation that she was worth a lot to those she helped.

After enjoying another morning with her coach, Anne gave Cathy a quick visit. "Hey cracked ribs with a 'C,' get released yet?"

"Wow, not even a 'how are you feeling today, Cathy with a 'C'?'" Cathy added, "Thank God you're not a nurse."

"I'm in a no-nonsense mood, so don't judge me and stop dodging my question. My comatose coach wants to know if you have received her forgiveness? Or, are you still whining about thinking you're not worthy? If you are, you just hurt her twice. Coach gets the runaway dog and sun glare, but not being full of yourself."

Cathy responded with the same seriousness, "Being released sounds nice, but I can't. Just not a fit. My life has nothing to show that I really deserve it yet."

"That's a poopy excuse," Anne shot back. Then she remembered her father talking about forgiveness. "This is all about your arrogance. You want your stupid queen to feel good about herself, to feel like she earned it. Forgiveness is a gift. Get over it."

Cathy stared at Anne in disbelief. "Look, little miss 'poopy excuse,' who is judging whom? Yesterday you're nice, today you blast me. Put a little gunpowder on your eggs this morning?"

"I am trying to tell you that you've got a crybaby queen destroying your life." In a mocking voice, Anne mimicked Cathy, "'I can't accept something that nice. I am too big of a loser.' Your pompous queen wants to brag on how great she is so she can feel like she deserves it. But, frankly, nothing she does will ever bring Coach back. So, stick her ugly butt in the dungeon or I am taking the orchid back."

"Hang on, you privileged little brat. You have no idea of the hell I've been dealt my entire life."

"No matter how slummy or gorgeous your world is, the self-absorbed queen will destroy it. No queen can really love someone with a love that gets their pillow soaked with tears and snot. She is like a nurse that goes around saying, 'Kiss my ring, you needy bozos.' Stick her in the dungeon and let her complain her sorry butt off."

Incredulous at Anne's rudeness, Cathy went on the offensive. "Explain to me, oh wise one, who still sits in her daddy's car seat, how does being a nurse and serving others make me a self-absorbed queen?"

Anne thought for a moment. Then, remembering how her father described how some girls love boys out of an unhealthy need to be loved, she answered, "You're stuck serving others mostly for your sake, not theirs. You're empty and hope they will fill you. You give because you need something back. But they can't fix what has happened to you any more than you being nice to people will change Coach's coma. I am telling you, it all starts when you humbly accept being released and stop trying to pay Coach back."

Both paused in thought, but Anne was far from finished, "Your ghetto queen will never help others freely. She will go psycho-nurse on ungrateful people. For nice people, Mary

Poppins shows up, but when you help a man like your dad, you will turn into the Wicked Witch of the West. Gotta let it go. People go nuts carrying the shame you're carrying."

Cathy responded in deep thought, "The only time I feel a little better about myself is when I help others. I never considered my need to be needed as unhealthy."

Not satisfied, Anne turned the heat up another notch. "You're helping sick people in an attempt to not feel like dirt. It's insane. You can't pay the debt you owe to one person to a different person and call it even. Every day your sorry queen is working to pay off a debt she owes to my coach by being kind to some other random person."

Anne, remembering her father teaching her about sharing the forgiveness he gave her, added, "And, I don't mean to pile on, but this week I learned about needing to have something in order to give it away. If you don't receive Coach's forgiveness, you will not have it in you to give it to your mom and dad. Not just them, but all your past and future idiots." Anne took a deep breath, "Well, cracked ribs with a 'C,' one more time. What will it be? Let go or get dragged?"

Cathy stared at the orchid showing rust marks, but she also noticed a promising new bud appearing. "Life is too short to live in misery. I will accept Coach's offer on one condition."

"What's that?" Anne asked, now smiling.

"Well," Cathy grinned, "I need you to be my snotty-nosed teenage coach."

"I only know what my dad and coach taught me."

"Good," Cathy looked at the clock and requested, "I need you to come back in about twenty minutes."

"Why twenty minutes?"

"I think my stepfather and mom need to receive an old beat-up orchid. It's time two more buttheads got released."

"Oh, yeah! Stick that whiner queen where she belongs. I am shocked by your nerve to set them free!"

Cathy, feeling free already, smiled and replied, "Bet you didn't think cracked ribs with a 'C' had the ovaries for it!"

Anne laughed so hard she ran into the bathroom to avoid having an accident.

Summary

Low self-esteem is often mistaken for humility. The truth is, low self-esteem results from measuring our domain and feeling like our domain looks embarrassing compared to others. Low self-esteem results from the injured pride of a humiliated ruler. They live frustrated, wishing but not having what others flaunt.

The same low self-esteem turns into arrogance when we measure ourselves against someone else and we come out looking better. But arrogance knows a very annoying friend—time. Self-esteem is always fleeting because everyone knows our impressive domains can unavoidably crumble apart in a heartbeat. The next phone call, a routine physical, the economy, war, a drunk driver, or one act of violence, or time itself. Everyone's confidence in their "living large and in charge" secretly lives in fear of losing what they have.

Arrogance rejects being forgiven freely. Prideful people believe their goodness easily offsets their badness. Conversely, few understand why someone who judges themselves as unworthy to receive forgiveness freely is also arrogant. "God resist the proud, but gives grace to the humble" (James 4:6).

Someone who rejects forgiveness until they make themselves worthy is still prideful. They just want more time. "My goodness will eventually make me worthy. Then, forgiveness is no longer a gift but a payment due to me."

Pride is offended by receiving something for nothing. Even the "ghetto" ruler hates the humble beggar feeling. Injured pride must first boost up the king or queen to look better. Paul reminds us in Second Corinthians 10:18, "For not he who commends himself is approved, but whom the Lord commends" (see also Proverbs 14:12; Isaiah 64:6; Matthew 9:10-13; and Romans 4:1-5).

Biblically, Christ's cross is our only source for forgiveness and His forgiveness is only received by those who humbly admit to their need beyond their ability. *To say, "I accept God's forgiveness," and then add, "now I must forgive myself" is just the self-appointed judge trying to redeem their pride.*

What source, other than the cross, can anyone find forgiveness to forgive themselves? Going to cut your finger and shed some of your own blood? What added work must you credit to yourself that adds to the work of the cross? What arrogance to think that the cross covers some sins, but not our particularly bad sins, and we must make up the difference. "For by grace you have been saved through faith, and that not of yourselves; it is the gift of God, not of works, lest anyone should boast" (Ephesians 2:8-9).

The humble person takes full responsibility for their wrong, points to the cross, and says, "I agree with Your judgments of me. It was me who did those awful things, not me on a bad day. I bring nothing of value to earn Your forgiveness. I accept Your release of all my sin and shame."

A proud person says, "I am really not that bad and I can prove it. I will do some very impressive things to restore my opinion of myself. Then, I can forgive myself and walk shame free because I earned it."

Self-earned forgiveness causes upper hell. If someone believes they can actually earn God's free forgiveness based on their goodness, they will require the same payback from others before forgiving them. But most people don't care if they are forgiven and rarely will anyone work for it. Unforgiveness only torments the person who won't forgive and they will accumulate a long line of names on their "I am still angry at these idiots" list.

To keep the list from getting even longer, they must build walls to protect their domain. Their fear keeps them from loving freely again. *Only those who receive God's forgiveness for free can give it for free.*

One's self-esteem, whether high or low, is born of measuring domains. Nonstop competing and comparing. Winning some comparisons, losing others. The driving nature compelling our need to do so is the king or queen's pride. The cure? First replace rulers and then you will switch domains to focus on. Serving Christ's domain offers freedom. "The Son of Man did not come to be served, but to serve" (Matthew 20:28). "Come to Me, all you who labor and are heavy laden, and I will give you rest…for I am gentle and lowly in heart" (Matthew 11:28-29). "Love…does not seek its own" (First Corinthians 13:4-5).

13

Unfair

Opening Thoughts

The way God builds and destroys our domains feels a lot like the luck of the draw. "The Lord gave, and the Lord has taken away" (Job 1:21). What will our next season be, feast or famine? God's blessings or God's wilderness?

Feast and famine are the circumstances God uses to mature His kids. The test is to keep our eyes on pleasing Christ, not on our gain or lack. *Sadly, there are many more who cannot handle His blessings than can handle His wilderness. Their eyes slip off the Giver and onto the gift. "Were there not ten cleansed? But where are the nine?" (Luke 17:17).*

Either we imprison our selfish ruler or our selfish ruler imprisons us. When we imprison our ruler, our purpose for living "I gotta do more to improve my domain and also protect it," transforms into "I have the ability to please the heart of God and He especially loves it when I impress Him. What happens materially afterwards is immaterial. What happens inside when God is flowing through me…that alone becomes worth living and dying for."

As our hearts morph into the heart of God through our obedience, obedience becomes its own reward. It is not that God is enough for us to live alone with on an island, but because He works through us towards others, that love we now thrive on becomes enough. We prosper on the fuel He made us to run on: His kindness, forgiveness, giving, gentleness, etc. Oneness with God first, then with others, is our reward (Philippians 4:10-18).

Our entire life comes alive when God rules. Relationships, work, nature, our five senses, purpose, eating, sleeping, and even the clouds in the sky all possess a richness we didn't know existed. We realize our old ruler's argument, "How can God expect me to trust Him mentally blindfolded?" is really just an absurd notion our inflated intelligence fabricated. (Proverbs 15:16; Matthew 6:21-34; Philippians 4:11; First Timothy 6:6-9).

Anne's Story: Part Nine

At three o'clock that afternoon, Anne witnessed the most inspiring event in her life. Her heart burst with excitement as she watched Cathy, with her bed tilted upright, tearfully explain her terrible accident to her parents and how Coach Cato laid comatose in the next room. She shared when Mr. Cato gave the orchid to Anne and how Anne also gave it to her with the words, "I release you." By this time everyone standing had tears dropping to the floor.

Cathy looked intently at her parents and acknowledged, "Things weren't that good between us growing up." Then

Cathy, still holding the orchid with her hands now shaking, handed it to her mother and stepfather. "I want you to know, I am sorry for my part and…I also release you for your part. We are all good. No bad history."

Anne stepped back in shock as Cathy's parents sobbed and hugged Cathy. Cathy's forgiveness released a flood of guilt. That Anne had something to do with the freedom they experienced gave her a deeper sense of joy than all her volleyball wins added together. She smiled, "It just doesn't get better than this. Another pillow soaked with tears and snot."

Anne quietly slipped out to leave Cathy and her parents alone. Sitting on the "Ambulance Only" curb, Anne finished eating a chocolate bar while waiting for her father to pick her up. She thought about the many seemingly incidental decisions it took to get her to this point of changing someone's life. Little decisions like getting pizza and spending the night. And boldly going into Cathy's room to see how she was doing. Feeding her dogs. Oddly, none of those small acts seemed like much at the time, but each was required to lead to the next.

Anne giggled to herself as she recalled her nagging fear of losing her precious happiness if she obeyed her father's "easy to please, hard to satisfy" expectations. "So," Anne reasoned out loud, "it comes down to there is a lot I don't understand about what really makes life worth living. A bunch of little things matter, some hard, some easy, but all significant. The queen never chose any of those little things because she just does what serves her." As Anne took another bite, she giggled, "I think this chocolate tastes even better with the queen locked up."

Anne's father finally pulled up. Before she put her seatbelt on, Anne exclaimed, "Dad, this experiment is taking on a life of its own." Anne's father quietly grinned as she excitedly recounted all the details of the reunion of Cathy's family. "And this is the strangest part. I just ate my favorite chocolate bar and somehow it tasted better today than ever before! And look at those bright, fluffy clouds…I think clouds are underrated…"

Anne's father chuckled and then interrupted her as they pulled into their driveway, "Anne, I have something to show you that I think you will like. It's behind the barn." Anne's father brought her around the back of the barn and after pulling the tarp off a beautiful, red sports car, he sighed, "I figured you would need this puddle-jumper for your new non-paying job at the hospital. These trips are wearing me out." With that, he tossed her the keys.

Anne jumped into his arms and thanked him with a big hug. Anne questioned, "What did I ever do to deserve such a fantastic car?" and then added, "I was just getting ready to apologize for how rotten I have always treated you. I'm ashamed I was constantly a taker, never thinking about you."

"I know, but you just opened up another side of me. I asked you to forgive someone like I forgave you and you did. Now, because of your obedience, I get to do what I love doing probably even more than forgiving. I really love giving."

"You're saying that my forgiving Cathy instead of hating her made you this crazy-stupid extravagant?"

Smiling, Anne's father explained, "Absolutely. My nature is unfair to forgive those who don't deserve it and also unfair when rewarding those who impress me by surpassing my 'hard to satisfy' expectations."

"Yeah, a good kind of unfair," Anne nodded while adoring her new car.

Anne's dad added, "Unfair works for me and that is why the queen must stay in the dungeon. The queen is big on unfair just as long as it is to her advantage. She will spoil everything that makes your life worth living."

Anne admitted, "It's all backward. I always considered your ways weak and boring. Queen Anne convinced me you were the enemy."

Looking at her father, Anne confidently smiled, "So, to get my mind wrapped around your parenting approach, I simplified it."

"Really?" Anne's father responded curiously.

Anne summarized as her father listened intently, "Your parenting boils down to me doing these three things: flow, go, and show. It works like this. All the time your kindness flows from you to me and then to others. Then, sometimes you tell me to go and do something special that would make you pleased. And the best for last, what really impresses your heart is when I look to do something over the top to show you how much I want to please you."

Grinning, Anne's dad returned, "Very clever. That also works for me."

Feeling empowered, Anne continued, "So, what other 'hard to satisfy' stuff you got? I eat this stuff like chocolate. Tell me you have more difficult challenges than Cathy?"

Anne's dad smiled with a tear in his eye, "You make me proud to be your father."

Summary

Although taking your neighbor out to lunch "just to chat" may seem like an incidental decision, lunch must take place first to make way for the next step that follows. Each act of obedience sets the stage for the coming act. At any point it could be the next act that changes the course of someone's life. All the while our hearts are imperceptibly turning into something more like God's heart.

The same is also true for seemingly incidental acts of evil. "I can't stand that man!" If fed again and again, that angry little monkey on your back will grow into a gorilla and eventually it will not settle down when told. In time, anger controls the heart, making it altogether dark and unlike the heart of God. The stage is set for violence. The next event becomes the straw that broke the camel's back. (Ephesians 4:26,27)

Summarized succinctly, we flow, go, and show. God's nature, like rivers of living water, flows out of us as we learn to walk out what He has worked in. Sometimes God moves on our hearts to specifically go. "Time to sell your business and minister to people as only you can."

As God never takes away our flavor freedom in our obedience to flow and go, He also gives us an opportunity to express our God-given creativity to impress Him. How incredibly delighted the heart of God must feel when one of His kids goes the extra mile to prove to Him their level of commitment to love Him back with the same quality of love He first loved them with.

So many Christians over-spiritualize walking in the will of God. Conveniently, they spend little or no selfless love, piously waiting on the Lord until He tells them to do a specific thing. Sadly, they miss the opportunity to use their freedom to flow in His selfless nature every day to everyone they meet.

What would God say? Perhaps, "Did I not give you the ability to envision and do amazing things? Why do you love it when someone you care about impresses you with their thoughtfulness? Impress Me with yours."

God loves a cheerful giver because He is one (Second Corinthians 9:7). The forgiveness of the cross is a means to an end—living in oneness with Him. Living one with Him, God gives His good gifts as "unfairly" as He gave us His grace. He really loves to give, which is why He expects all His children to be givers as well as forgivers. Jesus claimed,

"It is more blessed to give than to receive." Acts 20:35 (see also Matthew 7:11, 19:29, 25:31-46; and Luke 18:30).

Does God enjoy giving more than forgiving? Forgiving deals with removing the offense of a disobedient but repentant child. That's bittersweet. How much more delightful to give generously to an obedient child? God is generous to all, but imagine how thrilled He becomes when a child matures from needing forgiveness to fully investing their lives to pleasing His heart?

What honorable parent allows themselves to be out-given by their child who goes above and beyond what is expected of them? What loving parent doesn't want to give disproportionately to thank their child for filling their heart full of joy? "When you are living to impress Me, you can count on Me to give you whatever it takes to make it happen and to reward your labor of love." When we live "all in" to honor Christ with our lives, then James 4:2, "you do not have because you do not ask," applies (see also Luke 6:38).

God may not reward us in the "same coin" that we gave in. His kids may show their love many different ways (i.e. giving money, time, energy, dreams, comforts, safety, etc.). God rewards their obedience as He deems. He may thank someone who gave their time with more time, or give them a very full life in a short time. He may allow a difficulty for His obedient child to reveal to others the selfless quality of their love for Him, giving His child a greater fullness of Himself as their reward. God decides how to bless His kids (Hebrews 11:35-40).

Sadly, His heart is often broken for not being able to give as generously as He desires. How many of His kids are truly trying to impress Him by their total abandonment to Him? Further, how can He give to a person who will selfishly use the gift, or quickly take their eyes off the Giver and put them on the gift? Are we fit containers for God to bless, satisfied with simply pleasing His heart, not pursuing a payoff?

The only quality of love that God can reward constitutes His own selfless love flowing through us. We must first throw our ruler in the dungeon before living Christ-ruled. At that point, He changes our motives from selfish to selfless. We walk out what He has worked in. Then, in our conforming to His loving nature within us and yielding to His specific direction given to us, topping it off with our eagerness to impress Him, we will live in oneness with Him and we will absolutely love our lives. "I have been crucified with Christ; it is no longer I who live, but Christ lives in me" (Galatians 2:20).

And our heavenly Father proudly proclaims, "This is My child in whom I am well-pleased."

Part Three:

Freedom Truths

The following section explores many of the truths previously touched on.

The truths are summarized briefly, leaving room for the reader to pursue more Bible study and to ask God for greater revelation.

14

Flavor Freedom

God is a God of choice. "Choose for yourselves this day whom you will serve." "For whoever does the will of My Father..." God may be described as a "gentleman."

Not only does God not destroy our will, but we never lack for willpower. "If I only had more willpower" is a feeble excuse to avoid being responsible. Our will wins every time. Name something you chose to do or think that your will did not win the fight? Love decides which ruler our wills choose.

When our hearts decide whose will our will will serve, we simultaneously decide whether we will reap lower heaven or upper hell.

Do you struggle believing in free will? Do you think God's foreknowledge causes us to make decisions? If so, why would Satan, who was once God's "Chief Executive Angel" over all creation, tempt Christ to avoid the cross? Of all the predestined events throughout history the cross ranks as the highest. Obviously, Satan thought Jesus had a choice (Ephesians 1:4; First Peter 1:20; Revelation 13:8).

Jesus did not answer Satan, "Why are you wasting your time? Did you forget? The cross was decided before the foundation of the world and I don't have a choice." In essence, Jesus replied, "I choose to obey the will of My Father." Christ's choice was real. In the garden, Jesus sweat bullets, proving how real (Matthew 4:1-10).

Our heavenly Father also gives us freedom to make choices on our spiritual journey together as we walk out what He has worked in.

Flow

The primary and continuous way we obey the will of God for our lives is by yielding to His nature. However, before talking about how God gives us freedom in exercising His nature, taking a quick course on the "Dust and Deity Made One" basics is critical to lay the groundwork.

With His Spirit dwelling within us, our hearts are under new management. He is our new "want to," the driving desire to love selflessly. Jesus called it being "born again" (John 3:3). The primary application of the work of Christ's cross is the implanting of God's Spirit within, *enabling us to produce a totally different quality of love that meets His compatibility test.*

Conspicuously, wearing our own crown causes an irreconcilable compatibility issue. Our independent nature cannot produce a selfless action that pleases the heart of God or sets us free (First Corinthians 3:5).

Because the Spirit of Christ dwells within us, His character is not mimicked by us like a groupie mirrors their rock star idol. Christ's character is not closely counterfeited like printing fake money. Our goodness is not snow piled on manure or a veneer. Believers don't "fake it until they make it." With the Holy Spirit dwelling within us, He makes His thoughts and attitudes well up inside of us—the essence of oneness.

The flow starts carefully, but grows very naturally. Imagine having your cell phone always on an open call, listening to the voice of God. Or, the phone receiver off the hook. In essence, "Pray without ceasing." As we go through our day, we say to the Spirit, "Interrupt me anytime You want." Or, "I know how I am thinking, but how do You want me to minster to this person's needs?" 1 Thess. 5:17

And ever ask someone, "Can you smell that? Is someone cooking something?" They answer, "Yeah, now that you mention it, I do smell that." Or question, "What is that odd sound?" and someone answers, "Oh, now that I listen carefully, I do hear something." *As we heighten our physical senses when we intentionally focus, we heighten our spiritual hearing when we intentionally focus on hearing the Spirit's leading.*

Starting with the challenge of warring against our old thinking, we must pay careful attention to the Spirit as He directs us how to love others His way. Walking in the Spirit is a spiritual exercise, and our walking muscles gain strength through heightened listening and obedience, not self-reliance. Romans 8:4-9

With time and obedience, His new nature becomes our first nature. His selfless love becomes an expected flow, like "rivers of living water" (John 7:38). Jesus taught that He courses through us like a large grape vine flows life into a small branch and produces fruit (John 15:1-8).

The idea is something like that of children that naturally pick up the traits of their parents whom they trust, but often without realizing it. As a healthy person is not conscious of having good health, a mature believer is rarely thinking of their spiritual health. They just naturally produce fruit that represents their spiritual Father: love, joy, peace, kindness, etc., and enjoy their benefits.

Conversely, a sick person is painfully aware of what hurts. A spiritually sick person feels the annoying pain of living in upper hell. They bear the fruits of fear, anger, self-pity, jealousy, etc., all acting as God's merciful indicators that something is spiritually wrong on the inside. Something like the physical pain of a bleeding cut that acts as a merciful alarm to get our attention and our need to attend to it before it gets worse. Spiritual pain indicates we are wearing our crown, making decisions from the wrong "want to."

The character qualities God gives us are all found in Christ and include: honesty, generosity, self-control, forgiveness, encouragement, patience, kindness, meekness, humility, and many others (Galatians 5:22-23). Believers possess all of Christ's attitudes in them as if in a large holding tank, ready to overflow as needed. Since the Spirit of Christ is our infinite source, showing kindness or forgiveness never runs dry as though being drained out from the bottom.

Now the question, "How can believers still enjoy flavor freedom while yielding to the nature of Christ in their lives?"

When a yielded believer encounters a co-worker with a need for kindness, and the Spirit confirms, they instinctively think of a unique opportunity to show it. God's nature flows through them as they ask, "The weather is terrible. Can I give you a ride home so you don't have to walk in it?" Then, God gives the believer freedom to drive a particular route, stop to pick up something for their passenger, or stop for a cup of coffee. They talk freely about whatever things honor God. God gives them freedom to creatively live out His nature.

Put another way, perhaps you have an estranged friend who became very ill and is awaiting treatment in the hospital. "Show mercy" unconsciously dawns on you. *"Would visiting my friend honor You?"* "Yes, of course." Then, God gives you the freedom when to visit, to share a verse, talk about healing the past, possibly pray for peace about a known fear, or pray for their physical healing.

God gives us creative abilities that well up within us as we meditate and imagine. He meant for us to use all our God-given capabilities to follow His heart. Imagine how He must smile as He watches His kids ingeniously investing themselves in representing Him. All unique, all taking baby steps toward delighting the "easy to please" heart of God.

Go

The second way we understand God's partnership in our journey together is far more consciously driven. God is God and He can reveal His specific direction however and to whomever He desires.

God's promptings may come through His Word, another person, an experience, a dream, or a thought that powerfully compels us. We refer to these instructions with phrases like, "God is leading me," "God is calling," "God is impressing upon me," "I feel compelled by God," "I have a check in my spirit," "God's still, small voice," "I have God's peace about it," etc. (John 10:3; Acts 2:17, 9:3-20, 10:3-20; First Corinthians 12:8).

As with flowing in His nature, before we can listen to God's specific leading, we must truly want to know and yield. Our hearts require prep work performed by God's Spirit before we possess a willingness to hear God's direction. His Spirit first searches our hearts to expose selfish attitudes that will drown out His voice. A selfish heart will never voluntarily hear or surrender to God's selfless directions. His specific leading will never contradict His Word (Psalm 19:12, 139:23; John 15:3).

How does God give flavor freedom in following His specific instructions? Let's say after praying about what to do to please Him, God develops particular thoughts in your mind to start a program for the elderly shut-ins in your town to enjoy a heartwarming Thanksgiving dinner. That constitutes His specific leading. To carry out His leading, He gives you freedom to choose the location, the menu, adding entertainment or a gift, and taking pictures. That is using your God-given creative abilities to make God smile.

Now, in addition to using your resourceful abilities, suppose someone comes up after dinner and asks, "Do you mind if we take the leftovers to a young family in need?" Are you free to show God's kindness to a different group of people that were not part of His specific "elderly shut-ins" purpose to begin with? Can you deviate or is God rigid on His calling?

Jesus stated His Father sent Him specifically to the "lost sheep of the house of Israel" (Matthew 15:24), but He ministered many times to non-Jewish folks as they asked Him (Matthew 8:5-13; Mark 15:21-28; John 4:9-40). Jesus fulfilled His Father's calling and along the way obeyed His Father's nature by showing love and mercy to all who He felt compassion on. He even had enough compassion for a desperate wedding party to change water to wine, having nothing to do with His specific mission (John 2:3).

In the same way, Paul proclaimed God sent him to minister to the Gentiles, but he also freely ministered to Jews along the way (Acts 18:6-19; First Corinthians 1:13-17).

Simply put, God is excited to see His kids reveal His heart to everyone. He allows loving "detours" to those fulfilling His specific direction.

Show

Far beyond our ability to reason how it's possible, once our hearts' desires are truly focused on pleasing Him, then we can impress and delight the heart of God by taking the initiative in loving Him back. "Amazed," "well-pleased," and "takes pleasure in" are some of the emotions that are ascribed to God and Jesus (Psalm 149:4; Proverbs 15:8; Zephaniah 3:17; Matthew 8:10; Luke 12:32; Hebrews 10:38).

In other words, we can make the heart of God leap with joy. How? When we get our hearts in a place where our only desire remains doing what pleases Him, then go beyond His initial leading and impress Him with our eagerness to love Him back, God's heart does backflips.

Is it really possible that we have the capacity to "marvel" Him with how committed we are to loving Him back selflessly? God proudly bragged to Satan about how Job truly loved Him, that Job's love was pure (Job 1:8, 33:26). Job's faithfulness was not driven by anything selfish or even by God's specific leading. God boasted about him for his determination to live faithfully.

Paul states in First Corinthians 15:58 that we are to be "abounding" or going overboard in our work to please the heart of God. Paul summarized the extreme nature of Christ's love for us by His death and resurrection. Now, with the power of the cross within us, we also have the ability to go overboard or above and beyond in our love back (First Thessalonians 3:12).

What kinds of things would bring delight to the heart of God? "The Thanksgiving dinner for lonely old folks was a good start, but now I see the need for these lonely folks all year. I am going to pursue finding families in town to adopt them as their 'grandparents' and have them over for family holidays. That would make the heart of God beat happily."

....

There is nothing suffocating or tyrannical when walking with God. All His "guidelines" that we must stay within, His nature, are given to us out of love. And, within those guardrails, we will absolutely love our lives. We are no longer heartlessly bound by black ink on white paper. Or merciless laws.

Our hearts change after experiencing His heart. We don't serve a threatening God because we already possess and spend His loving heart on obnoxious people. If God has not transformed our hearts, then we work like a miserable child that is asked to clean up their room. They moan and groan over picking up each piece of clothing, making an easy job seem like torture (Hebrews 10:15-18).

Our purpose in life embraces the highest and most fulfilling purpose possible…pleasing the loving heart of the Creator of the universe by loving others selflessly. Oneness in, oneness out.

Our Struggle

Once we understand these truths, our difficulty is not whether God indwells us, or leads us, or gives us freedom in obeying Him. Instead, our conflict pivots on whether we really want to obey a Father who directs us to spend His selfless heart. We often want the blessings His incredible nature has to offer us, but we cringe when we're impressed by Him to offer His selfless love to others.

Selfless love costs our domains too much.

As a last resort, instead of surrendering control to gain His peace and joy, we upgrade our selfish management style from making stupid and painful evil decisions to making smart and self-serving good decisions. At all cost we avoid asking Christ for His leading or heart. The "phone call" has ended. No open line.

We walk our paths alone in our goodness. We wrongly believe we can skip His selfless "flow" and just move on with our own self-driven "go," and even our prideful "show." Our labor, however sacrificial, remains in vain (Genesis 16:1-16; First Corinthians 3:1-15, 13:1-5).

Many wrongly assume that God is after our surrendering our badness to Him and He is done. Not even close. That is just the whining "queen or king" trying to avoid the dungeon.

God wants oneness with us which requires His cross-quality love flowing through us. Our hearts must first surrender to Him before He can birth His selfless nature in us, then He in turn controls the quality of goodness that we produce. "He who glories, let him glory in the Lord" (First Corinthians 1:31).

On the other side of obedience, we fully enjoy our lives. Nonetheless, the Holy Spirit cannot ignite His amazing purposes in our lives if we quench the Holy Spirit's fire in our lives. 1 Thess. 5:19, 2 Timothy 1:6

15

Easy to Please, Hard to Satisfy

The principle, "God's heart is easy to please, hard to satisfy" brings clarity in understanding how God lovingly rewards our small steps of obedience while encouraging higher expectations on us. Simultaneously, God's love praises our slight improvements and His love equally desires nothing less than perfection for us.

Wrongly assuming God is "impossible to please" as opposed to "easy to please" turns Him into a cruel tyrant. If a child attempts to please their parent but is put down with demeaning criticisms such as "Your efforts embarrass me," "You always disappoint me," and "You failed me again," they typically project the same heartless and critical parenting on God. All their attempts at being good are driven by a fear of rejection, instead of driven by love. Nothing they do is good enough. They serve a mean ogre and resent it (Second Corinthians 5:14).

No person or country can rise above their understanding of who God is. If they believe God is harsh and heartless, then they become hard to please and make those around them miserable with their condemning religious attitudes. They sit in harsh judgment of those who are not as devoted as themselves. Beliefs differ but true love is universally easy to please, or it is recognized as oppression and resented (Proverbs 22:24; Matthew 23:15; James 1:20).

Further, believing God is "easy to satisfy" instead of "hard to satisfy" will also abort our growth toward being like Christ. If a child's parent placed very low expectations on them, they are trained to give up easily. Comments like "It's your life, mess it up if you want," "You passed and that's all that matters," and "Do as little work as you have to" illustrate the problem. So, at the first sign of difficulty, they throw in the towel. Our selfish nature only adds to the problem. "If it doesn't affect me, I don't care."

Compromise rules the heart with a voice that says, "Giving it my all is far too much to ask." When they pray, they presume God is indebted to them for whatever halfhearted goodness they accomplished. When God doesn't reward their lazy efforts, they fault God for being unfair (Luke 14:33; Acts 7:51; Ephesians 4:30; Hebrews 10:29).

Understanding that God's heart is "easy to please, hard to satisfy" produces both encouragement and responsibility equally. We enjoy the comfort that God's heart isn't waiting until we reach the top of the mountain of perfection to recognize and reward our little steps up the hill.

Being hard to satisfy, God will never give up on helping us to rid our lives of our sin nature. Much like a merciful doctor must be hard to satisfy as he tirelessly removes all the cancer from their patient (John 15:1-7).

How is God Easy to Please?

Remembering the outrageous price that Christ paid to give us the opportunity to take on His selfless character and live one with Him, imagine how elated He must be when His kids take one small step toward walking in oneness with Him! God is a "rewarder of those who diligently seek Him" because He first diligently pursued us. His heart is for us and every little step of our obedience is His heart's reward for the huge sacrifice He made (Matthew 20:1-16, 25:29; Luke 19:23; Hebrews 11:6).

There is an important distinction that we must understand. This distinction will in turn explain how a perfect God can be easily pleased with our humanly feeble and imperfect attempts at pleasing Him.

The distinction relates to the source of our goodness: Me in me or God in me? Can we please God's heart by bringing our goodness to the table? Or do we please God by our yielding to His love within us (Romans 7:18)?

Right being must precede right doing. A perfect God can't reward what isn't compatible with His pure nature. It doesn't honor Him for someone to act sacrificially kind if they do so desiring to serve themselves. (First Samuel 15:22, 16:7). There is nothing we can do, with a selfish quality of love, regardless of how great the sacrifice, that pleases God. "Though I bestow all my goods to feed the poor, and though I give my body to be burned, but have not love, it profits me nothing" (First Corinthians 13:3).

However, God is pleased when our small steps of selfless obedience are driven by our desire to simply put a smile on His face. He actually enjoys seeing Himself poured out through us. Our proof of His pleasure traces back to source availability. Only God in us produces selfless (agape) love.

The action itself may appear feeble. God enjoys the yielded heart behind the effort. God doesn't need a superstar "ringer" because He desperately needs anyone's help with correcting the universe. And, He loves the blessings that come into our lives and others as we place obeying Him as our chief desire (Matthew 10:42).

If God puts on someone's heart to call a hurting friend or pick up a piece of trash and they obey, they become absolutely lovable to a perfect Father. "Absolutely?" Really? Sounds a bit extreme for a perfectly holy God to absolutely love a greatly flawed person.

God is not compromising His holy standards in the slightest degree to proclaim, "My heart enjoys seeing Bobby speak one considerate word toward the woman he always had contempt for. I completely love seeing Me in him, even if Bobby has a very long way to go in so many other areas."

As Jesus prayed for oneness hours before His cross, imagine how elated He feels when the work of His cross accomplishes what He so urgently prayed for. Since our thoughts and actions are born of oneness with Him, He is justified in rewarding our small steps of obedience without compromising His pure nature.

Our growing from selfish to selfless is typically very slow and we often fight mixed motives. Helping someone we can't stand naturally starts as a nasty struggle within. We may even question ourselves. "Is our obedience love-driven, reward-driven, or guilt-driven? Are we begrudgingly obeying? Or maybe avoiding God's punishment?"

The Holy Spirit will reveal to us that our hearts are a mixed bag of motives. Some motives are converted to pure because God's selfless nature compels them, but some motives aren't transformed yet because our sin nature still has us blinded and trained to want a payback.

God is not shocked. He sees Himself in us even if we are very disappointed in ourselves. Rest assured that He still loves our baby steps. God even enjoys our hard fought decisions to serve Him over our petty idols and habits. When, on His leading, we put down the bag of potato chips, turn off the movie, arrive early to church, smile at a stranger, and pick up someone else's trash, we are pleasing Him. (1 John 4:20)

At the beginning of our spiritual journey, loving God is simply the choice we make in the face of our competing desires. The question is not what we really, really, really want to do, but if we decide one more "really" to obey God. Jesus calls that love. His heart is pleased when we finally yield to Him after a long line of selfish decisions. Jesus stated in John 14:15, "If you love Me, keep My commandments" (see also Matthew 6:24).

"Feelings make great shipmates, but terrible captains." God is not surprised that we often make decisions driven by feelings of fear, anger, envy, and guilt. But emotions, by themselves, have a very poor sense of direction, usually straight into the rocks. God wants to be our Captain, staying on the course His nature and truth sets.

After we decide to obey His leading, not before, His shipmates come along to assist. He fills our hearts with the emotions of lower heaven (i.e. joy, peace, contentment, hope, love, etc.). As our Captain, simply deciding to forgive one insensitive remark puts a smile on the heart of God, bringing us His peace that replaces our anger (Galatians 5:22-26; Colossians 1:10).

After obeying the heart of God by returning kindness to someone who caused us evil, we clearly recognize something more powerful than ourselves is at work in us. We know we are not behaving anything like our old self.

In time, what was once "really, really, really" difficult obedience becomes our first nature instead. Our hearts intuitively know that what attracts His pleasure is seeing Himself in us. To God, when one of His kids return kindness for evil, they supernaturally become absolutely lovable. "Christ in you, the hope of glory" (Colossians 1:27).

Someone may contest, "But what about our part in submitting to pleasing God? Don't we get some credit for that?"

When we behave in a manner that is pleasing to God, we choose to obey both a desire and a power that He implanted in us to begin with. We can't take credit for a "want to" and a willpower that we could never possess apart from His Spirit living in us. Paul reminds us in First Corinthians 4:7, "What do you have that you did not receive?" (see also Luke 17:10 and Philippians 2:12-13).

The argument for taking credit is tantamount to a grandfather clock demanding of its maker, "You know how amazingly beautiful I look and that I keep perfect time. I deserve special treatment. I want a wall all to myself, without any other pictures to draw attention away from me. And, being so beautiful, I deserve frequent polishing."

The clockmaker incredulously responds, "What do you have or what can you do that you do not first owe to me?" Like God said in Job 41:11, "Who has preceded Me, that I should pay him?"

We must humbly realize the complete monopoly our selfish hearts possess over ourselves. Paul said it best in First Timothy 1:15, when he admitted, "Christ Jesus came into the world to save sinners, of whom I am chief" (see also First Corinthians 15:9). If we proudly feel as though we merit God's favor, we are still operating with a self-righteous motive that disables the "flow" coming from Him.

When God blesses our goodness that flows from Him within us, He typically calls our reward a "gift." When a person lives their life selfishly, their consequence is labeled a "wage."

Wage verses gift. Gifts are free, wages are earned. "For the wages of sin is death, but the gift of God is eternal life" (Romans 6:23).

Why "wages"? Selfishness requires work. First, they straight-arm the Holy Spirit. Then they work through the bitter upper hell emotions that follow managing their domain. Their most painful work entails suffering through the frustration that living selfishly causes in their relationships. Selfishness erodes oneness, destroying the greatest yearning in their life.

God is a God of choice. To remain self-controlled, they want to work alone. Instead of receiving God's heart and yielding to His selfless "want to," they actually labor for the misery they earn and what they subsequently will receive. In their self-focused goodness, they bitterly make comments like, "No good deed goes unpunished" and "No one appreciates me" (Matthew 12:32; John 16:8; Acts 6:10, 17:24-28; Romans 1:17-23; Second Peter 2:15).

How much credit can someone take for deciding to exchange their bondage for Christ's spiritually rich life? After tasting the appetizers of upper hell, who in their right mind would turn down the gift that offers a friendship with their Creator and brings freedom?

Only a person with so much self-confident arrogance that they think they can outsmart their Creator or, sadly, they developed an appetite for the initial entrées from hell and think they will also enjoy the main course.

Imagine how God's heart must backflip with excitement when someone does so little as to agree, "I am a mess. I need Your help. Please make me right with You." Jesus eagerly responds to the thief on the cross, "Today you will be with Me in Paradise." Luke 23:46.

Christ's love for His Father and for all mankind drove Him to His cross. Our surrendered hearts, each and every step, constitutes the sweet reward Christ anticipated while being nailed to His cross (Luke 15:10; Romans 1:32; First Corinthians 6:9-10; Second Peter 2:1, 3:9).

How is God Hard to Satisfy?

The Pharisees taught the crowds, "Do not do unto others as you would not have them do unto you." Then Jesus came along and removed three little words: "Do unto others as you would have them do unto you." In doing so, Jesus makes known His Father's hard to satisfy expectations.

By framing the statement in the negative, the Pharisees' axiom meant, "I don't want you to hurt me or steal from me, so I won't hurt or steal from you. You stay on your side of the fence and I will stay on mine. Don't expect me to help you and I won't expect you to help me." Lawful, but loveless.

However, stated in the positive, Jesus' teaching means, "Since we desire others to help us with our problems, then help others with their problems. Since we want forgiveness, then we must give forgiveness. Since we desire others to speak kindly with us, then speak kindly with them." Then Jesus added in Luke 14:13-14, "Invite the poor, the maimed, the lame, the blind. And you will be blessed, because they cannot repay you" (see also Matthew 5:43-48, 25:31-46).

How is God's heart hard to satisfy? He wants His perfect love to flow through us. God desires our love for others to reach far past obeying His laws ("You shall not steal"). He is after our hearts. "Give your hard-earned money to help your sick neighbor who stole from you." And, to give without seeking recognition or personal gain. Where else but from His Holy Spirit can we get His quality of love? Who else could receive the credit? As Paul stated in Second Corinthians 5:14, "For the love of Christ compels us" (see also Matthew 6:14-15; Romans 5:5-8; Ephesians 4:28; and First John 1:5-7).

The three-letter word "all" in the greatest commandment, noted in Deuteronomy 6:5, sums up God's demanding desire for complete purity in our love for Him, "You shall love the Lord your God with all your heart, with all your soul, and with all your strength" (see also Matthew 22:37 and Mark 12:30). Not "most of the time," or "as much as you want," or "what others can see." Perfection is what God is after because anything less would be unloving, from Him to us (John 17:23).

This "new" and "greatest" commandment operates much differently than all the old "Thou shall not" commandments in the Old Testament. As we selflessly obey God's leading in us, all the other commandments are subsequently obeyed and surpassed, not from duty but willingly out of love. A person with a selfish love can wisely obey, "You shall not steal," because they don't want to get into trouble. But to obey His new commandment, God may direct you to invite your "co-worker from hell" over for dinner, requiring a relationship with Christ as your source for His selfless love.

When someone sponges up spilled milk and the sponge is then squeezed, out comes milk, not lemonade. When we "sponge up" the quality of love that God possesses, out of us God "wrings out" His same quality of love toward others. In fact, none of God's attributes are capable of being hoarded by a believer who is yielded to His Spirit. If and when someone who claims to walk with God doesn't "wring out" His character, they violate His "all." "If we love one another, God abides in us" (First John 4:12).

The second commandment is, "love your neighbor as yourself." The "love your neighbor" relates to the "wringing out" of God's love to those around you. But, what does the "as yourself" refer to? We must first love ourselves? How so?

Jesus prefaced the second commandment, saying it is "like" the first. What is in the first commandment that is brought forward into the second? Or what is now loved in "yourself" that you pass on to your neighbor? You only have two choices: God's *selfless* love in you, or your *selfish* love in you.

"Like" the first means the second commandment is a re-gift of the first, using the same source to share the same quality of love. If the first commandment is obeyed, then the second follows automatically.

The two commandments come together like this: God requires me to serve Him with all my heart and entire life. The only reason I can is because He enables me to by first giving me His heart. Then using the same quality of love He and I share, I then share it with others. They get introduced to Jesus through me.

The love that we love within ourselves, that we share with our neighbor, is the love that now brings life into our lives.

To help us with "all," God painfully yet mercifully reveals any area in our lives where we are still clutching onto our domain, maybe money, agendas, time, body, work, family, dreams, stuff, or reputation (Romans 2:4; James 1:2-7).

16

Where the Love War is Fought

Many churchgoers have been taught that the battle for obedience begins in their minds. Consequently, they believe better biblical understanding remains the critical element required to tip the scales in the areas they struggle to obey God.

They listen to "renewing your mind" sermons for hidden keys in hopes of winning the battle in their heads. Some try memorizing Bible verses and then claim those same verses when they are hit by temptation. Others attend special weekend conferences and read books to try to win the conflict in their minds.

In the greatest commandment, God always orders the "heart" before the "mind" and "body" because the decision to love is always determined first in the heart. Our hearts choose who we love, self or God. Our love decides our master, not a lack of information. Our defiant hearts are the culprit, not "If I only knew better." Our minds only back our hearts' decisions. Our bodies respond to our minds' orders. That is the naked truth that few actually want to admit.

For example, when our hands shovel French fries into our mouths, it is because our minds directed our hands to. To stop our hands, we don't take out a hammer and punish our hands.

When our minds ordered our hands to eat greasy fries, it was simply following orders also. Our hearts made the call. "I love yummy fries." Our brains are not at fault any more than our hands.

If our hearts chose not to love greasy, salty food, then they would command our minds to order our hands to throw the "nasty" French fries into the trash. Our hearts decide.

Finally, the decision our heart's make reflects the boss our hearts choose to serve.

Subsequently, our hearts' greater love for greasy, salty food has the ability to order our minds to memorize, "I can do all through Christ," as our hands stuff French fries into our mouths.

Our minds possess an incredible ability to rationalize our hearts' desire to remain self-ruled. Our minds back our hearts' "play." Here are some common excuses our minds come up with to justify our hearts' desire to entertain disobedience. "No one will ever know I am lusting." "Coveting is a victimless offense." "I am just thinking about it, not doing it." "I deserve it for as little as I get paid." "I used to be so much worse." "I am doing better than…" "I will make it up later."

All our mental rationalizations are given the "green light" by our hearts. Hence the wise axiom, *"Never underestimate what the human mind is capable of rationalizing apart from the Holy Spirit revealing our hearts."*

God is not insulted by the tug-of-war we experience when choosing who we love in our hearts. He simply wants to know if we will choose Him over all opposing loves. Serving our domains pulls hard. God will not trick, manipulate, scream, dangle a carrot, or razzle-dazzle us into loving Him. God could no more tempt us to love Him by encouraging selfishness than un-god Himself. "If anyone desires to come after Me, let him deny himself, and take up his cross daily, and follow Me" (Luke 9:23).

Jesus refers to the irony that exists when we attempt to serve God for selfless reasons. "For whoever desires to save his life will lose it, but whoever loses his life for My sake will save it" (Luke 9:24). God's hard to satisfy expectations set us free. On the other side of our difficult obedience we will absolutely love our lives. We experience lower heaven here and now. Knowing that, how could a loving Father insist on anything less than perfection?

A note of explanation:

Second Corinthians 5:17 reads, "Therefore, if anyone is in Christ, the new creation has come: the old has gone, the new is here." NIV

Many people like to add the "all" in this verse, as the KJV did in 1611. "All things have become new." Inferring, our hearts are made completely new, leaving only our confused minds to transform. "All" is not in the Greek text. Ironically, Paul starts the next verse with "all." "All" was on the tip of his pen. If Paul wanted "all" in verse 17, why didn't he add it?

Are we honestly going to blame our lack of understanding truth caused us to sin? We meant to love God back but we were confused? Even Paul (Saul), when he persecuted the Christians, knew in his ignorant zeal he was kicking against the goads. Acts 26:14

Romans 12:2 states, "Do not conform to the pattern of this world, but be transformed by the renewing of your mind."

This verse comes after Romans 8, telling the reader to walk in the Spirit, not the flesh. After we choose our new Master, we must transform how we think. Our old covetous hearts ordered our minds to go through great lengths to figure how to steal without getting caught. Then, our obedient hands and feet made it happen.

Now, Spirit lead, our hearts tell our minds to go through great lengths how to figure out the best way to help someone in need. New training for a new Boss. Our minds calculate the best method of solving someone's nightmare. Then, our hands and feet make it happen. (Ephesians 4:1-32)

17

All For Oneness

The strongest yearning in our lives embraces enjoying oneness with another. To love and be loved. To walk through the fire together. Equally, the greatest grief we experience constitutes the death or rejection of someone we experienced oneness with. Jesus wept when He witnessed what torment the death of a loved one inflicts on our souls (John 11:35).

When we experience joy, we eagerly share it with someone we are close to because in doing so they magnify our enjoyment. "I got your joy in my heart." When we suffer great pain, it becomes bearable, as though reduced in half, when shared with someone we love. "I got your pain in my heart." Oneness constitutes the most fundamental need of our lives. Without oneness, we endeavor to fill our void using many substitutes: food, alcohol, work, entertainment, sports, and pleasure. Yet all fail.

Why oneness? Why is it so rare?

By God's design we inherently hunger for oneness. "Let Us make man in Our image" (Genesis 1:26). The "Us" and "Our" refer to the unity of the Father, Son, and Holy Spirit. The three-in-one. Tri-unity. Tri-oneness. We crave oneness because it constitutes God's design in Himself that He gave to Adam and all his descendants. A plural oneness. (Genesis 3:22; Luke 1:35, 3:22; John 3:34, 14:16, 15:26).

The same Hebrew word is used for marriage, "and the two will become one flesh." Two becoming a plural one. Two that unite so intimately that they treat themselves as one (Genesis 2:24).

Yet if it's so essential, then why is it so rare? When sin entered, our spiritual oneness with God was broken. Our hearts became independent, divided from God and consequently divided from each other. In-divid-uals, or, in a "divided state." We lost His quality of selfless love. We still yearn for oneness, but our selfishness makes us "all elbows." Our selfish ambitions interfere, causing arguing, fighting, divorce, etc.

Jesus died to restore oneness. The at-one-ment. Christ offers His selfless nature to all those who want to reunite with God as their spiritual Father. To do so, Jesus took our selfish sin nature on Himself, breaking His own oneness with His Father on the cross. "My God, why have You forsaken Me?" (Matthew 27:46). Broken divine oneness shook the earth. Conquering the power of sin, proven by His resurrection, Christ overcame our spiritual separation. Oneness was restored. "I am ascending to My Father and your Father" (John 20:17).

Anyone can walk their path alone and speak to God as their far-off Creator. Even Satan speaks with God as his Creator (Job 2:1-6). But, if anyone desires to walk in oneness with God and speak with Him as their own Father, they can only do so by applying the work of Christ's cross. "I am the way, the truth, and the life. No one comes to the Father except through Me" (John 14:6).

Every doctrine throughout the Bible points to oneness with our heavenly Father and then, generated out of our oneness with our Father, oneness with each other. Many Christians miss this critical truth and make worshiping the principles and doctrines of the Bible their highest goal. Consequently, they sacrificially dedicate their lives to obeying principles to live by, not a Person to live with.

It is a tragic error to think that eternal life is God's gift that we must wait to receive after we die. Eternal life begins as we walk together with Him in oneness today, talking about what pleases His heart. He shares His quality of love with us and we re-gift it to others. God is our new spiritual Father and walking partner. Walking arm-in-arm we experience a preview of heaven (John 17:3).

Many avoid oneness with Jesus to remain self-ruled in their goodness. It's so much easier to obey words on a page, not someone who examines their hearts. Ink is easy to fool. We can keep a critical spirit when making encouraging comments to someone (First Thessalonians 5:11; First John 4:11).

A principle, purpose statement, Bible verse, or doctrine cannot go on walks and share joy, suffering, love, or give calm assurance in a storm. God's children that experience eternal life now, eagerly read His letter and ask for His direction. Christianity is Person-driven. His Spirit also reveals our hidden sin attitudes that a verse defines but we have always ignored. And, being one with Christ, He implants His selfless (sinless) character in us to live out the Biblical principles He reveals. "Search me, O God, and know my heart" (Psalm 139:23).

Christ's cross was a means to an end, oneness with God, not the end itself. The greatest honor anyone can give Christ's cross embraces applying His sacrifice by walking in oneness with Him. In doing so, they will reveal His great love to others. Simply looking up to His cross and mournfully thanking Christ every day for His great sacrifice, but stopping short of walking in oneness with Him, causes a spiritual breakdown that breaks the heart of God. Satan must find the spiritual disconnect exhilarating.

What Does Oneness With God Look Like?

Oneness first yields to the nature of God, stating, "What pleases You, pleases me. What breaks Your heart, breaks mine. What You think is beautiful, I think is beautiful. What You have the time for, I have the time for. What You think is entertaining, I think is entertaining. What thoughts You want me to think, I want to think. Who You forgive, I forgive." In other words, God's heart becomes our heart. We get on His page, not Him on ours. "Let this mind be in you which was also in Christ Jesus" (Philippians 2:5).

As we become one with His heart, His nature pours through us. All the character needed for our obedience originates from Him. His forgiveness flows through our hearts. His patience runs through us. His gentleness is my gentleness. His love streams through us. We are not merely a close imitation or a representation of Christ. To others it looks like we mirror Jesus, but we actually become Jesus with skin on (John 17:22-26).

What's the difference? A supervisor who represents or mirrors his boss, shouts, "The boss is coming! You better stop messing around. He hates poor work habits."

On the other hand, a supervisor who possesses their boss' attitude says, "I hate poor work habits. Stop messing around or find a new job." Oneness takes on the heart of God. The way God works is how I work. Jesus is never away. Oneness never shouts, "Jesus is coming. Look busy!" (Acts 16:14; Romans 8:2-16, 12:2).

18

True Repentance

Many cry their eyes out after committing a sin that shatters their lives. They "repent" in their terrible pain, but a week later they recalculate the consequences for the same sin and figure out a way to minimize or remove the pain. Not surprisingly they "fall" again. What makes repentance stick?

When living in oneness with God, our desire to please Him becomes our reason not to entertain sinful thoughts or give in to temptations. Avoiding negative consequences is no longer the criterion we base our thoughts and decisions on.

The heart of God doesn't change a week later, or ever. Neither will new favorable consequences affect our repentance. "I finally figured out how to win at the card game at the casino." Emotional rationalizations won't sway us either. "But premarital sex with this guy is different. He loves me and we will work through the other stuff."

Minimizing painful consequences ceases to be the issue when we understand that God dwells within us and enjoys our friendship. Choosing to lie or not isn't about potential pain. Nor is it about disobeying a verse written on white paper. It's about breaking a heart.

When people on the Jenny Craig diet cheat on their personal diet plan, the Jenny Craig diet is not offended because Jenny does not live in them or personally care.

Christians often follow the Bible like they follow a diet. When they cheat a little on the "diet plan," they are not overly concerned. They rationalize that it is just a minor cheat that can be made up with a little more exercise. It is just a little lie, a slight offense, harmless gossip, or a justified theft that our "make-up" goodness cancels out.

We must realize that sin wounds a heart that wants the best for us. A friendship is strained. "Do not grieve the Holy Spirit" (Ephesians 4:30). When we realize that repentance is first about not wanting to break the heart of God, not merely breaking a rule or avoiding painful consequences, we stop rationalizing our sinful thoughts as if there were no wounded parties.

True repentance hits a person when they decide to no longer break the heart of God. "If God doesn't want me to gamble, I don't want to gamble. Nothing changes that."

As someone takes on Christ's heart towards others, old temptations lose their appeal. Just like a spouse's loving devotion can ruin their spouse for all other competing loves, God's fulfillment in our lives ruins our desire to look anywhere else. Our souls become captured and spoiled for what only God can offer. God succors us with Himself.

Previously, we may have envied the success of others. Now we cherish a far richer success and feel sorry for those, rich or poor, that don't enjoy it. Nothing competes with walking in oneness with the nature of God. (Matthew 5:29; Second Corinthians 12:9-10, Second Peter 1:4).

Nathan Intervention

God sent the prophet Nathan to shock King David into owning his offense. Over a year after the adultery and murder, still hiding in his sin, Nathan confronted King David with a story that forced Him to acknowledge the seriousness of his offense. Finally, King David truly repented. (Second Samuel 12:1-15)

Amazingly, with King David's spiritual relationship with God, it took a third party with a clever story to shake David out of his denial. Maybe he thought about all the men he sent into battle that never came home. Maybe he reasoned any woman he wanted was rightly his. Solomon sure did. *Whatever the case, David's heart remained unrepentant.*

The first lesson. We may think a person's sins are obvious to them, but our fleshly hearts can subtly order our minds to put to work its amazing talent for rationalizing. Many times, it takes an intervention for someone to "acknowledge" the pain they have caused by hearing and seeing it on the faces of those in front of them. Even a "man after God's own heart." (Eph. 4:18)

A second lesson. Don't be afraid to be a Nathan if God tells you to. Nathan did David a huge favor, risking his life.

A third lesson. Don't think you are too spiritually mature and beyond being conned by your fleshly heart. Listen, with no heart of your own in the matter, to what God wants to tell you and invite other's wisdom. (Galatians 6:1)

A fourth lesson. God accepts sincere repentance, even when late, and after confronting, and from a person who knows better. A lot better. (Psalms 51, 32)

19

Choosing a Father

You have probably heard, "You can choose your friends, but you can't choose your family." Natural family, true. Spiritual family, false.

Everyone chooses their spiritual family by choosing one of two fathers to submit to. Each father parents using a very different quality of love. One creates oneness, the other brings division.

If a person loves from selfish motives, they may pay little or no regard to Satan himself, but nevertheless chooses Satan's style as their default parenting. Driven by their birth nature, they prefer Satan's "be your own boss to get what you deserve" maxim. Christians, desiring to obey their heavenly Father, operate from Christ's selfless love (Romans 8:14-21, 9:8; First John 3:7-10).

Understanding the difference between choosing Satan's fathering and God's fathering requires placing several pieces of truth together. This section comes together slowly, like a picture puzzle becomes clearer as all the pieces are in place (Galatians 4:5-6).

Parental Rights

Lucifer is the spiritual father of self-rule. Lucifer rebelled against his Creator to rule over himself and all creation. We read his words in Isaiah 14:13-14, "I will exalt my throne above the stars of God...I will be like the Most High" (see also Ezekiel 28:13-19). Lucifer's arrogance led him to believe he could out-wit God as to governing His creation, so he attempted a mutiny.

In his rebellion, Lucifer (a.k.a. Satan), persuaded multitudes of angels to follow his lead. Satan also persuaded Adam and Eve to take "the bite" that promised them the opportunity to be their own boss (Genesis 3:4-5).

By joining Lucifer in his revolt, Adam and Eve became spiritually separated from their Creator and part of Lucifer's family. By their choice to rebel, God lost full custody and Lucifer became their new spiritual father. After Adam and Eve elected Satan for their spiritual father, all their descendants inherited their spiritual genes. Consequently, everyone is involuntarily born into Satan's spiritual family and receives Satan's self-ruled nature (Ephesians 2:2; First Peter 2:9; First John 3:8, 5:19; Revelation 20:2-3).

The consequences of Adam and Eve choosing Satan as their new spiritual father gave Satan sole custody rights. Subsequently, all mankind experiences both spiritual separation from their heavenly Father as well as physical death.

God received His parental rights back over all mankind when Christ redeemed mankind. By His death and resurrection, Christ overturned Satan's legal custody. Jesus did for mankind what mankind could never do for itself. Before we can be placed back into His family, we must respond to His invitation of adoption. The pivotal decision remains choosing His fathering over Satan's. When selecting God as our new Lord, we choose selfless love as our new nature. "The kingdom of God will be taken from you and given to a nation bearing the fruits of it" (Matthew 21:43).

We don't add a second father. We rebel against Satan much like Adam and Eve rebelled against God. We rebel against Satan's headship and join Jesus' family, thereby taking on His family likeness. We're told by the apostle John in First John 5:18, "We know that whoever is born of God does not sin; but he who has been born of God keeps himself, and the wicked one does not touch him" (see also Romans 8:14-17; Second Corinthians 11:3; Hebrews 2:10-15; and Second Peter 2:1).

Christ's cross and resurrection gives everyone the option to choose a new spiritual Father and then to walk in oneness with Him. Satan loses his control and no longer can legally force us to obey him as our spiritual father (John 17:21; Philippians 2:15).

The Nature of Satan's Self-Rule

The key players in the lineup that represent Satan's family likeness include: self-rule, selfishness, pride, self-righteousness, independence, rebellion, and control.

As our spiritual birth father, these qualities also represent how Satan treats us as his children and not surprisingly, many prefer it-like a young child that loves visiting their father because he spoils them. They do and eat what they want, stay up late, and live irresponsibly. Are fallen angels any different? (Second Timothy 2:26).

The Bible says all mankind inherited self-rule. No one needs to teach a child to say, "You're not the boss of me!" Or to want to take another child's toy with dozens of other toys available. We are born clutching onto our crowns, hoping to gain any level of control as we see best for ourselves. And, as the two-year-old adamantly screams against someone hundreds of times smarter and bigger than they are, our foolish tantrums with God are far more ridiculous. Adulthood doesn't diminish our sin nature (Romans 5:14; First Corinthians 15:22).

We prefer being our own boss because we are driven by one relentless desire: to serve ourselves for selfish fulfillment. "I may hit some potholes, but being self-ruled is a must in order to live a little selfishly. I can keep my party under control…."

The self-governed person rejects God's parental authority and consequently must rely on their own wits, direction, and character to get the absolute most out of their life. As long as their life is running smoothly—without people problems, or financial problems, or health problems, or marriage problems, or legal problems—they feel they are doing a competent job of being self-ruled.

On smart days it's, "Do for others because you want them to do for you." On ambitious days it's, "Whoever dies with the most toys wins." On frustrating days it's, "Eat, drink, and be merry for tomorrow we die." On mean days it's, "Do unto others before they do unto you." On noble days it's, "Do for others to build my opinion of myself."

Meanwhile, all the days remain godless. Satan offers several options when things get ugly. Get revenge. Get stoned. Denial. Depression. Hate. Stress. Strive for control. Guilt. Never open your heart again. Escape. Medication. Etc.

When governed by Satan's nature, there are no days where it's said, "My father from hell takes great interest in my struggles and gives me wisdom and strength to find peace within the storm." Or, "I know my dear dad has a loving plan. I can trust him with my finances and to meet my needs." Or, "My guilt is gone. Now I can forgive others and live free to love again." Or, "This body is not for long. I look forward to my new one and sharing eternity with a father I can trust." Or, *"I can't love them, but Satan can through me."*

Exposing Godless Self-Rule

We participate in a hostile spiritual war between two fathers, each vying for our souls to choose the one against the other. By continuing in self-rule, one reveals they prefer Satan's parenting traits of arrogance, rebellion, control, and selfishness. Choosing self-rule makes several outlandish assumptions about one's ability to control their life and their wisdom to figure out how best to live (Second Corinthians 6:14; James 4:4).

If we're being honest, most of us are happy to make one more right decision than wrong decision. As we look for our lost keys, we argue with God over how to operate the universe using our vast intelligence. We confidently trust our formula for living will make us happy, ironically, as we drive to our therapist (or the bar). Have you ever asked yourself where such insane confidence comes from?

It is obvious we are delusional about our true ability to control our lives. Most of us will forget even a short list of items just by walking through the door and into the store. What causes our anxiety and stress? Trusting self-control over God-control is foolishness gone wild (Proverbs 13:10; Luke 12:25-26).

Does living self-ruled offer freedom? In one sense, yes. Having only one voice to obey—self—serving oneself is without any contest. You only possess one desire so there is a freedom to simply pursue your wants.

But that one desire also holds you hostage with a nagging compulsion to keep getting better for yourself and to constantly figure out how. It will invariably put you in a trade war with all the other people who are driven by the same compelling need to enjoy more. Will they trade fairly or will they cheat you? Some jerks will con you by giving you less than they agreed. Many are happy to take far more than they give or just steal. Some are givers at first and then demand their selfish expectations later.

How Self-Rule Chooses

If someone rejects submitting to God, they choose Satan's spiritual family by default. But how can Satan be their father when many don't act very evil?

Remember, the name of the forbidden tree in the Garden was the "tree of the knowledge of good and evil." Not the "tree of evil." Good and evil come from the same tree, just not God's "tree of life." Eating from the tree of the knowledge of good and evil meant, "I choose the same independence Lucifer chose. I want to be in charge, not God. My capacity to remain in charge is paramount."

After choosing Satan's family tree, picking either good fruit or evil fruit is a secondary decision. "I make good or evil decisions with a 'what about me' little voice jabbering in my ear all the time." We choose good or evil based on how we feel at that moment. Typically, how we feel relates to how we evaluate each decision best serves us (Genesis 3:1-6).

Which appears the most favorable for each situation? Patience or impatience, mercy or judgment, generous or stingy, honest or dishonest, faithful or unfaithful, lazy or industrious, etc.

These are the kinds of questions self-ruled people must try to calculate correctly. "If I take her out to a really nice dinner, will she give me what I want? Maybe a relaxing evening, or a sense of value, or sex? Will it help if I am honest or dishonest about my last relationship? I wonder if a thoughtful gift will tip the scales? Maybe I will need to get pushy or buy a little extra alcohol to get what I am really after?" I, I, I. Eyes turned inward. Myopic.

In many self-governed relationships there may be fairness and harmony on the surface, but oneness and trust in the relationship remains paper-thin. Everything Satanic remains selfish and necessarily weakens oneness, eventually divides, and breeds distrust.

Imagine the bride that vows, "I recognize that to be fair this relationship has to work for both of us. I promise to love you with all I am, but you need to also meet my needs. All bets are off if you disrespect that give and take. Or, if you lose your health, or can't make money, or for any other reason you are unable to scratch my back when I scratch yours."

What else can selfish thinking base its decisions on but to give and take equally, or to cut back on the giving until it becomes fair? How long before fighting, manipulation, jealousy, envy, and unfaithfulness dominate the relationship?

You may be thinking, *What about a wise self-governed relationship? Both partners know to pick only the "good" fruit. They also sensibly recognize that giving over 50% at certain times is inevitable and it should come back later.*

If so, then enjoy these vows: "We both have strengths and weaknesses. We are a good match to help each other through tough times, unless of course one of us gets stupid stingy and things get too lopsided or unfair for any reason. I don't mind being patient, but I must be honest. I am not going to live forever and I want to enjoy what happiness is rightfully mine. At some point, if you don't deliver, I will call my backup relationships that promise better."

Even though making allowances for each other's weaknesses, selfishness looks into the mirror and plainly states, "life is short and I deserve to be happy." Selfishness has an unfair threshold. Looking for greener grass becomes the next challenge.

Being Christ-ruled yields oneness with God as our Father and then with each other. All relationships flow from having received His quality of selfless love which is found only on His "tree of life." To serve, not to be served. To forgive with a gift. To walk through the fire together, as an honor. To rejoice when others rejoice, to cry when they cry. To encourage others when they're defeated. To give to those who cannot give back. To hope the best for others. To step in front of a bullet intended for someone else as Christ did for us on the cross (Matthew 22:39).

Satan's "Angel of Light" Deception

Have you always just assumed the only two options for the argument, "What is mankind's birth nature?" was between good and evil? Did it ever enter your mind that the chief question to answer is "Who is mankind's spiritual father?" Why not?

Our spiritual father decides our motives, whether selfish or selfless. Our father's motives drive everything we do. What difference does it make if what you do is good, if it remains just as selfish as someone acting evil? Remember, same tree, same father. "Whoever is born of God does not sin" (First John 5:18).

Good and evil are the wrong two options for deciding our birth nature because they bypass the prior "Who am I influenced by?" question. "Who inspires my motives? Who is coaxing my heart and what is their character? Who is tempting me to choose to be honest or to lie? Who inspires these thoughts that just dawn on me? Where does this 'want to' come from?"

Lucifer prefers the conflict to remain between good and evil because he wants everyone to believe the issue is about what you do, not the spiritual father your heart serves. *Lucifer diverts the question from "Who is our birth father?"*

by showing off the self-ruled person that lives nobly. "I am an atheist. I do not believe in God or Satan. But I am obviously a good person because I am spending my fortune trying to help people. It is all about being good, not religious."

The deception continues, "This kindhearted atheist is living proof that we don't serve a spiritual father. We simply choose good or evil. Evil is purely a bad choice, not a family trait. Evil decisions are clearly made by everyone: Christian, atheist, agnostic, Muslim, etc. *Education is the key to turning bad behavior into good behavior—no need for a new master" (Second Corinthians 11:14).*

20

The Rhino and the Flea

Time to learn how being "born again" into Jesus' family changes everything.

"SIN" and "HOLY" represent our two spiritual natures, and since they control our actions, they are capitalized. "Sinning" and "holiness" are their respective actions and remain in lower case because they are simply byproducts of either SIN or HOLY.

For example, Johnny's mother orders her three-year-old son, "Johnny, sit down in your chair." "No!" Johnny screams defiantly. Irritated, Johnny's mother commands, "Sit down, Johnny, or I will spank your bottom!" "NO!" Johnny adamantly returns, throwing his mac and cheese on the floor. Johnny's mom yells, "Ok, you don't get any ice cream! In fact, you are getting a spanking and going straight to bed right now." As his mom gets the spanking spoon, little Johnny sinks into his chair and mutters, "I may be sitting down on the outside, but I am still standing up on the inside."

Little Johnny was born innocent (because he hasn't had the opportunity to do anything), but he inherited Satan's defiance, what the Bible calls his SIN nature. Compelled by his SIN nature, Johnny commits actions (sinning) that everyone notices (like food throwing) and for which he gets disciplined. Being self-ruled is the defiant attitude within that goes unaddressed. Sinning gets all the attention.

Relative to the size of their spiritual significance, SIN (Satan's nature) resembles a rhino, and sinning is only the little flea on the rhino's back. Satan's grand deception allows our SIN nature to rule without much notice by directing our attention to the messy "food throwing." Even a self-ruled three-year-old is clever enough to sit down on the outside, while remaining defiant on the inside. Meanwhile, the rhino cunningly goes unnoticed (Luke 11:39, 16:15; Second Timothy 3:5).

What do you think matters more to your heavenly Father, the wasted food thrown on the floor or the rebellious heart that rejects His parenting? Stealing from work or the ungrateful heart that covets? Gossiping words or the bitter heart that despises another? Adultery committed or the unfaithful heart that wanted to commit it?

Have we cleaned up our actions, as though sitting down on the outside pleases Him?

Sinning causes problems. Receiving all the attention, everyone focuses on stopping evil behavior by education and administering painful consequences. "If people only knew the self-serving benefits of choosing good behaviors, we could all get along." *We kill the irritating flea, while ignoring the deadly rhino that tramples us.*

In essence, society, and often Christians, focus on behavior not motives. Our hearts remain self-serving when choosing to stop evil behavior. God is nowhere in the picture.

Very few people ask themselves why they stole when they knew it was wrong. "I stole from work. What is wrong with me that I want something that isn't mine?" Or, "Why can't I stop the craving to take the biggest piece? Why do I lie? Why do I love to gossip? Why do I enjoy seeing others in misery? Where do these mean compulsions come from? Why do I entertain cheating on my spouse? Why do I envy someone else's success?"

Even fewer people ask themselves why they act generously, honestly, and lovingly. "Am I kind just to get something back? Am I trying to feel good about myself? Do I have a return address attached on my goodness? If I was being truly generous without selfish motives, why did their ungrateful response upset me? And, even if I did expect something in return, doesn't everyone?"

Having a high opinion of our own goodness, the things we take pride in, is the reason we must always be Spirit lead. We ask Christ what He wants, not want we think we should do.

....

If serving our birth father never reaches a desperate level of pain, bringing awareness to Satan's parenting style, then why change spiritual fathers? Johnny learns to sit down on the outside just in the nick of time to avoid too much pain. His SIN nature remains in control, just wisely holding its breath.

Johnny learns how to pick the good fruit for selfish reasons. "Be kind to others and they will be kind to you." "Fight fairly to resolve your conflicts so both sides win." Satan's "Angel of Light" program deceives far more successfully than his "Angel of Destruction" alternative (First Corinthians 5:5; Second Corinthians 11:14).

Are those who claim to be God's children paying any attention to whether they are sitting down on the inside, or just the outside?

SIN and Sinning

Sinning is missing the mark, or stealing the tool. SIN is having the selfish desire within to want to miss the mark in the first place, or coveting. Missing the mark isn't an accident—SIN prompted it.

As long as someone's self-control over their selfishness can keep their stupid sinning down to a minimum (that is, avoiding adultery, fighting, stealing, breaching contracts, drunk driving, addictions, etc.), the person will never feel enough pain to reveal their need for a new father (Luke 11:21-22; Ephesians 4:18, 5:8, 14).

SIN and sinning are still just as offensive to God when someone picks the good fruit from Satan's tree. When someone is kind, driven by their desire to impress themselves or others, they are operating in Satan's world of arrogance and self-righteousness. They remain blinded, serving Satan's domain. *Nothing fails greater spiritually than self-serving goodness.* Jesus said in Matthew 9:12, "Those who are well have no need of a physician, but those who are sick" (see also Mark 2:17 and Luke 5:31).

Arguably, Lucifer wants his kids to rule their SIN nature wisely, making him proud to be their parent. "Be your own boss, but serve yourself wisely. Be fair and reasonable. Use moderation and keep your impulses in check. Whatever you do, don't act entirely foolish and find yourself crying out to God in a prison cell." His friendly voice sounds identical to our own until we are spiritually born again with a new voice coming from a new Father.

The Self-Righteous Spirit

Everyone knows that picking evil fruit, or stupid sinning, will likely catch up to them at some point and cost them dearly. Regardless, church lovers and church haters typically deal with acts of sinning differently.

Church haters typically measure their acts of goodness against their acts of badness. "I may lie to the government, but I don't break my word to a friend." "I am not as bad as those hypocrites." They try to keep their party under control to avoid the painful consequences of evil fruit.

Church lovers are taught they must get forgiveness from the cross for sinning itself. The actual lie stands out as our nasty offense, their deceptive heart goes unnoticed. "God, please forgive me. I keep lying."

For virtually everyone, SIN, what drives our sinning, hides in our blind spot. The spiritual father who motivated someone's sinning is rarely called out and confronted. Even for churchgoers, typically only the visible "food throwing" gets our attention.

Who prays, "God, I want to change my heart's attitude to Your heart's attitude toward the person I gossip about?" Or the car I covet? Or the sexy neighbor?

The flea gets all the attention while the rhino tramples believers into the ground. Why don't they realize their first and foremost problem is the particular tree they choose to eat off?

When they are invited into Christ's family, are they asked if they are willing to commit to the cost? *Grace is free, selfless love is not. Do they know that the Holy Spirit will give them a new selfless love that will war against their old selfish love?*

Or are they simply thinking to remove pain? They assume picking good fruit, but from the self-ruled tree, is serving Christ. They quit swearing at drivers on the road, but remain angry just the same. Some men may stop cheating on their wives and feel good about only daydreaming about cheating. A woman may stop picking fights with her husband, but remain just as cold-hearted, believing she has spiritual victory (Matthew 7:21-23; First Corinthians 13:1-4).

Some are very gifted and impress the crowds, but not God. The soloist can sing her lungs out, but all week long carry an attitude of resentment toward her husband. The elder works impressively expecting appreciation, but if it's not enough, starts criticizing those in charge. The ladies gossip in the corner with their study Bibles in hand. Upper hell is in full force in parts of the church while appearing so righteous (Jeremiah 17:9-10; Revelation 2-3).

………………..

Why doesn't the Holy Spirit make a lot of noise about Satan being the father of someone's motives? Why doesn't He scream, "Over here is your big problem! Satan is the one who tempted you to want to steal or look for applause. It's all about who drives your actions, not your actions!"

Many people that repent do so to get rid of pain, not to ask God to take over, or even to get His opinion on their sinning. Self-rule hopes to enlist God's help to reduce their pain from stupid sinning with no intention of surrendering to God. *It is not that the Holy Spirit doesn't speak, it's that self-rule turns a deaf ear to remain in charge.*

Self-serving repentance doesn't require God's selfless nature to replace damaging drug use with less harmful smoking. Then to replace smoking with less harmful overeating, which is eventually replaced with working out one's frustrations at the gym. Sadly, rarely is the anger, anxiety, and stress brought before God for His cure (Hebrews 12:15-17).

What about the person who believes they have truly repented by changing their outward behavior, yet remain oblivious to their selfish motives? "I am going to stop complaining at work and start saying nice things. I'm going to start using honey instead of vinegar." Or, "I am a Christian now, so I am going to start giving instead of taking and see if God turns my finances around." Or, "I am quite certain that being honest will get me noticed and they will give me that promotion." Such people remain deceived into thinking God is making the change as they grow in their outward religious activity, but not in their inward submission to God. Everything good is selfishly motivated. Where is the Holy Spirit then?

To those self-driven in their goodness and deaf to the Holy Spirit's voice, the Holy Spirit faithfully gives merciful warning signs.

SIN brings bondage: anger, arrogance, fear, self-pity, jealousy, stress, deceit, and fighting. Some stand back and ask, "If I am serving God's program, then why is it still so painful? Fear, anger, and self-pity just don't seem like God's way of blessing obedience. Something isn't right."

Others remain self-confident that they will valiantly forge through their bad days with greater self-effort. Even some pastors reason in their self-reliant efforts, "Building a church gets stressful...so many people to pacify and impress and keep motivated. The strain is brutal."

Even after feeling SIN's warning signs, the stubborn self-righteous double-down on their efforts to stay independent in their goodness. Going to God first with no heart of their own in the matter is never considered. *That would require relinquishing control of their goodness, the very thing they take pride in most and will give up last.* "At all costs, stay in charge, especially with your goodness. Achievement builds self-esteem."

Many reason that their stress is the necessary "yoke" that they must carry to produce God's fruit. They read, "Come to Me…take my yoke upon you….and I will give you rest." When asking themselves, "If I got Jesus' yoke, how come I got stress instead of His rest?" They answer, "Jesus must not be carrying His weight." (Matthew 11:28-31)

The confusion doesn't lie in the sharing, but in taking on weight that Jesus did not give us. The yoke figuratively referred to an individual burden placed on another, light or heavy.

The problem? Christians do not "Come to Me" first, to ask Jesus if He gave them the burden they painfully carry. If stressful, not His burden. If rested, meaning all the heavy lifting is done and time to enjoy the benefits, then yes. The same exact "rest" God enjoyed on the seventh day. "Wow! Now I get to enjoy My labor."

God didn't need a nap on the seventh day. He absorbed pleasure from His completed work. "It is finished." Much like preparing a meal for six days then feasting on day seven. Are Christians feasting on Christ's completed work? Or are they imagining Jesus threw that heavy load on them as if His work on the cross wasn't finished?

....

The Bible speaks of our SIN nature being able to grow in deception. The further one gets from the Light, the less visible SIN's presence is realized. For the same reason, religious leaders full of darkness (SIN), not the criminals or harlots ashamed of their sinning, easily justified their mock trial and crucifixion of Jesus. Jesus called them out in John 8:44, when He said, "You are of your father the devil" (see also Second Corinthians 4:4 and James 1:15).

Compounding the problem, where SIN is strongest, its presence is realized least. A man takes a drink and knows that if he has another, he probably should not drive. After the second drink he has just enough sense not to drive. After three drinks he confidently believes he can drive safely. If he slugs down four drinks, he stumbles out believing he can fly a jet.

Paul reminds us in Ephesians 4:18-19, "Having their understanding darkened, being alienated from the life of God, because of the ignorance that is in them, because of the blindness of their heart; who, being past feeling, have given themselves over" (see also John 12:40 and Hebrews 3:11-12).

Without going to God and asking the Holy Spirit to expose SIN, Satan, having the whole floor all to himself, makes convincing arguments to justify self-serving attitudes with good behaviors. *Never underestimate what the human mind is capable of rationalizing apart from the Holy Spirit* (John 8:38, 41).

Self-ruled religious people would never think to pray, "Father, tell me something I don't want to hear" and then wait patiently for His answer. They attend church, but grow spiritually backward, doing impressive good works without a heart that has even stopped to consider if it's actually submitted to God. SIN looks inconspicuous from the outside by picking good fruit and inadvertently letting others know. Many call this a "religious spirit" (James 4:1-7).

So what needs to be learned?

HOLY and Holiness

To remedy mankind's spiritual problem, Jesus needed to do far more for us than just forgiveness of sinning. We required a "new factory" to produce a completely "new product." Not a remodel, but a brand-new foundation. A new "want to" coming from a new heart. If God only forgave us of our sinning, but didn't give us the opportunity to choose Him as our new spiritual Father, then we would remain stuck in a vicious cycle of receiving forgiveness for our sinning and yet unable to choose a different master to serve. We may choose good fruit, but always be driven by selfish reasons.

Without a new Source, we remain condemned to continue sinning. God would not be justified in justifying us. Giving forgiveness without implanting His new nature amounts to snow piled on manure. Right being must precede right doing (Second Corinthians 5:17; Titus 3:5; First Peter 1:3, 23-25).

By Christ's death and resurrection, He took away Satan's custodial rights. "He who sins is of the devil, for the devil has sinned from the beginning. For this purpose the Son of God was manifested, that He might destroy the works of the devil" (First John 3:8). We are no longer enslaved to Satan's SIN nature and consequent sinning. Now we have the option to choose which father (or tree to eat from) that yields the fruits of either lower heaven (life) or upper hell (death). We have the freedom to be ruled by Christ's disposition, HOLY, thereby producing acts of holiness (Romans 6:15-19, 8:6-11; First Peter 2:25).

HOLY is our born again family "standing," imparted by His Holy Spirit within us, to produce all the fruit that Jesus produced. When prompted by His Holy Spirit, we operate in His selfless love that produces acts of holiness (i.e. kindness, gentleness, meekness, self-control, generosity, forgiveness, etc.). "But now having been set free from sin, and having become slaves of God, you have your fruit to holiness, and the end, everlasting life" (Romans 6:22).

Many Christians remain extremely frustrated and unfruitful. Not relying on Christ's selfless nature to direct them, all they know to do is constantly battle with their selfishness to act "kinder" than they really want to act. Their hearts hate the fistfight that occurs to obey God when He makes demands that don't promise selfish payoffs (Matthew 5-7).

What does it take to live under the influence of our HOLY nature?

The freedom that Christ offers by living HOLY is not found before making the decision to change families, which requires a conscious decision, or "counting the cost" of putting off Satan's family character qualities and putting on Jesus' family character qualities. We deliberately surrender our crowns. Just as Jesus was nailed to His cross in order to overcome Satan, we must willingly nail down our rights to serving ourselves on our cross to walk in victory over Satan. "For he who has died has been freed from sin" (Romans 6:7). "He who does not take his cross and follow after Me is not worthy of Me" (Matthew 10:38).

Those who refuse to die to SIN and falsely believe Christ will scoot over on His throne and allow Satan's self-rule to co-reign, will only experience more hell within. They live more miserably than an atheist who has only SIN as their ruler. Their selfish hearts will constantly try to barter with Christ's selfless heart. Christ will never allow peace. Inner turmoil will make them miserable and they will wear their Christianity like a splitting headache.

Tragically, too many churchgoers remain naive about dying to their SIN nature in order to obey their new HOLY nature. They focus on stopping evil actions and starting good Biblical behavior, while ignoring their motives in doing so. To them, Christianity is all about forgiveness, not a new relationship first. The flea outweighs the rhino by a ton.

In essence, they are stuck back in the same miserable decision-making position as anyone who doesn't believe in Christ's redemption. They decide which fruit is the most self-rewarding to pick, whether good or evil, both off the same self-serving tree. Just as Paul wrote in First Corinthians 1:18, "For the message of the cross is foolishness to those who are perishing, but to us who are being saved it is the power of God" (see also John 3:16-21).

To want the joy, peace, hope, and love that living HOLY brings, and to deliberately make the decision to actually submit to living Christ-ruled, remain miles apart. Our wills must surrender, not just hate the consequences of SIN's enslavements. "Come to Me, all you who labor and are heavy laden and I will give you rest." (Matthew 11:28).

21

SIN's Painful Enslavements

God gives plenty of agonizing warnings to all those who live naively or intentionally under Satan's parenting. His forewarnings are painful but merciful samples of lower hell (Hebrews 12:6).

Playing ruler isn't easy business. Instead of "God's kingdom come," it is my kingdom (or queendom) come. All governing decisions fall back on us as we are driven by an insatiable desire to acquire, control, protect, and impress. What else causes stress, fear, discontentment, anger, and distrust? All those are just the emotions from choosing the "good" fruit. When choosing the "evil" fruit—lying, stealing, fighting, cheating, etc.—the emotions get very ugly fast.

Let's look at a variety of the enslavements of living under Satan's fathering. Here are just a few of the many.

A rarely realized side effect of living to please oneself is the attitude projection that naturally accompanies it. If someone readily misleads others, they will quickly assume anyone who makes the excuse "sickness" for not coming to help them move, is lying. Someone who holds a grudge believes others also keep offenses, which causes them to continually look over their shoulder, expecting a nasty payback when they least expect it. Etc.

Whether actual or not, all the selfish intentions of their own hearts are suspiciously placed on others. Their world is full of "jerks" like themselves. When you think about it, living selfishly delivers a double whammy. A selfish person not only devises a way to get the biggest piece of pie, but they also suspect everyone else possesses their same "taker" agenda. "If I don't take it, someone else will" (Matthew 7:1-5; Romans 2:1-4; Titus 1:15-16).

Another nagging enslavement of selfish living is the constant comparing and competing. "How does my domain measure up to theirs? My car, house, spouse, intellect, future, body, clothes, appearance, etc. Do I compete, or does my world look slummy by comparison?"

When our domains don't measure up, we feel like losers and try to pick up our pride by winning in a different category. "I may not be as successful, but I am younger and better-looking than they are." Poor self-esteem results from losing, arrogance from winning, but neither brings freedom. Like Paul stated in Second Corinthians 10:12, "They, measuring themselves by themselves, and comparing themselves among themselves, are not wise" (see also Proverbs 20:6; Romans 12:3; and Second Corinthians 12:6).

The most painful oppression that results from living independent of God's rule relates to severe emotional disorders. The growing fear of our domains being destroyed drives much of these illnesses. Here are some obvious questions that reveal whose domain is being served, ours or Christ's.

If someone is looking over a high ledge, or in a crammed elevator, or driving on a suspended bridge, or in an intimidating crowd, whose domain is in trouble? When self-conscious about speaking, meeting someone new, or worried about the opinions of others, whose domain is the focus? When someone can't sleep for fear of losing their only source of income, or feel they are being watched, or believe others are talking about them, or afraid of bad news on the phone, whose domain captivates all their thoughts and drives all their fears?

When Christ is the ruler, we take on the attitude of Christ. What is His heart in the matter? Oneness states, "What Jesus fears, I fear. So, Jesus, do You fear crowded elevators? Jesus, do You fear hospitals? Bridges? Death? Jesus, do You worry about my income? Jesus, what is Your attitude about me developing a mental illness?"

There are no simple answers for overcoming anorexia, obsessive compulsive disorder, hoarding, bipolar disorder, depression, schizophrenia, self-mutilation, etc. Only God knows the internal struggles of each person and He alone judges the hearts of those who suffer from life-dominating conditions. And He, loving them to the degree of being one with them, painfully shares their suffering (Matthew 25:35-40).

However, there are obvious indications regarding whose domain is being worshiped by the person suffering from those disorders. Why not address the spiritual factors that God reveals as well as the other possible natural and childhood causes? Why not treat the whole person, majoring on God's remedy? Ask, "Whose spiritual family inspires that attitude?"

Often, when a child is hit by a terrible pain, the only option they can find to bring peace into their domain is by locating a manageable corner in their life to control. "I can't control what my abusive father does, but I can control whether I eat. Now I feel I have some say-so in my life." Or, "I will escape into a pleasant pretend world." Or, "I will clean (or organize, hoard, dream, fixate, self-medicate, etc.) to distract my mind from thinking about how upsetting the rest of my world is." Or, "I will physically cut myself (or hit, pull my hair out, burn myself, flip razor blades in my mouth, etc.) to try to mask the unbearable emotional pain of being severely mistreated."

For those overcome with such painful emotional problems, why not pray for windows of mental clarity and revelation as to whose domain is being served now? Then teach and model how to turn control over to Christ, a thousand times if necessary. How does His Holy Spirit want to govern their domain? "Give that desire for control over to Me."

How will they learn to think and live selflessly? "How does Christ want me to love that messed up person who abused me?" "How does Christ want me to forgive the wolves who raised me, destroying my youth with their foolishness?" The healing process is often lengthy, requiring a great deal of loving support from others that represent "Jesus with skin on."

Many experience the hopelessness that being "four drinks drunk" on SIN brings. Their continued anxiety and anger fed the cute little monkey until it grew into a 2,000-pound gorilla on their back. Living in upper hell is not what God wants for anyone. Christ's cross gave us power over our thoughts. After our hearts repent of living apart from Him, we are able to renew our minds with His truths. Often a laborious process, but so was feeding the gorilla.

....

Giving up our domains brings freedom from the constant second-guessing about whether decisions we made were personally profitable or not. Freedom of regrets over all our "coulda, woulda, shoulda's." Freedom from fearing that our next relationship will go up in flames. Free of the constant frustration of not getting the life we wanted. Free from the anger of unforgiveness.

Imagine being able to trust God in your spouse and they trust God in you. No more jealousy, coveting, or envy sucking life out of your marriage. Free from the depression that seeps in when your anger cannot be resolved. Free of the necessity to be a control freak. Free from competing with others or manipulated by what they think of you. Free from the fear of dying. Free (James 4:1-4).

But, as stated, wanting the blessings of surrendering one's domain to Christ and actually surrendering are two very different things. God's blessings only come on the other side of our selfless obedience.

The only part of God's nature that we enjoy is the particular part that we have obeyed.

22

No Belief Bias

When the doctor convincingly states, "This powerful new drug has proven to work wonders on virtually every patient with your symptoms," a huge number of people will swear they feel better even if the doctor gives them a placebo.

Everyone is prone to belief bias. We want something to be true so we imagine the effects that make it true. If someone is superstitious and spills salt, anything bad that happens next was "caused by the salt." Or, "If you wear this unique metal bracelet, you will have tons more energy," and amazingly, "I felt like I could run twice as far."

The phrase, "A sucker is born every minute," sums up how easily we imagine outcomes without any empirical evidence to support those outcomes. Brilliant and talented people included.

It is easy to laugh at other's belief bias, but ignore our own fabricated notions. Are Christians any different? Who is to say that Christians suffer any less from belief bias than any other religion? Are there any repeatable and undeniable outcomes regarding the Christian faith? Any evidence that mankind serves one of two fathers, each producing different and demonstrable consequences?

Experiencing the effects of upper hell and lower heaven requires zero belief bias. Living obedient to Satan's fathering or obedient to God's fathering offers real outcomes that everyone can attest to with absolutely no imagination.

What provable results does self-rule produce? Anger from unforgiveness is not a figment of someone's imagination. Fear over health problems or loss of wealth requires no pretending. Frustration caused by not getting your way causes many sleepless nights, evidenced by red eyes the following day. Depression from hating one's lot in life doesn't even have the energy to make-believe. Purposelessness is inescapable when standing in a cemetery, evidenced by the need to get a stiff drink to make life bearable again.

What provable results does Christ-rule produce? Those who forgive live free from bitterness and are able to love again. Those who trust their heavenly Father with their bodies enjoy peace when facing death. Those who don't get their own way aren't frustrated because they are seeking Christ's way to begin with. Surrendering control of life's difficulties to a loving Father brings hope. God's purposes bring strength and excitement to live aggressively in this world, while simultaneously revealing that breathing is overrated. Going to a funeral causes the deep sorrow of broken oneness, but that same sadness is made bearable knowing a loved one just graduated into perfect oneness with their heavenly Father, and one day there will be a reunion.

Each parent produces real results while we are still breathing. Nothing is fabricated out of thin air. The results are easily determined and repeatable, as much as any science experiment. Get 10,000 married couples and tell half to live selfishly and the other half to live selflessly for six months, then question them to see whose marriage grew stronger or weaker. The results are a forgone conclusion.

Two undeniable outcomes. Two observable attitudes that drive those outcomes. The Bible teaches that each attitude has a spiritual father behind it. Everyone is born with a self-ruled/selfish attitude and must be transformed to change into a God-ruled/selfless attitude.

It is a hard choice to lock up our screaming selfishness in the dungeon, but everyone chooses. God gives us multiple indicators that reveal which father we are serving. Appetizers of lower heaven or upper hell. "You will know them by their fruits" (Matthew 7:16).

In spite of the concrete evidence produced by obeying one parent over the other, non-believers can still choose to argue the personal nature of God. Whether God really indwells and flows through you, implanting a new selfless "want to." They argue that living selflessly is simply a choice of the will. No special born again nature required.

But will they attempt to live selflessly for a month to prove their point? No personal agendas, just serve others for their benefit? To truly hope the best for someone who harmed them? Or, freely forgive someone who offended them and then give them a gift? Or, be honest when it cost them to be honest? Or, give in secret to those who cannot give back? Or, start putting other's interests above their own interests? Who will guide and empower (parent) that quality of love?

What requires belief bias constitutes pretending there aren't two opposing natures and their respective effects. It isn't the difficulty of discovering the truth that people struggle with, it is surrendering one's life to Christ that they take exception to.

"Taste and see that the Lord is good; blessed is the man who trusts in Him!" (Psalm 34:8). It is not that God will not prove Himself as true if "tasted," it is that the world is not really interested in savoring selflessness. Everyone starts with an acquired taste for selfishness, giving us a strong belief bias against trusting God, even if He produces obvious outcomes we desire over the outcomes we settle for to stay in control.

Paradoxically, the very same person who refuses Christianity, stating belief bias, handles their inevitable upper hell experiences by rubbing a little belief bias on the pain. How?

If being our own boss remains non-negotiable, to continue our happy charade that we are making the right decision, we are forced to pretend all is good. "I will make-believe my self-serving lover is committed to me through any hardship." Or, "Life will get wonderful after I get my new car (or house, or job)." We imagine better results than we actually get when picking Satan's parenting. Expectation of gratification buys the car, but a month later disappointment drives it while we anticipate what else will make our life wonderful.

Further, picking the good fruit on the tree of good and evil will not bring true oneness with each other because all our kindness, honesty, gentleness, etc. remain driven by selfishness. Picking good fruit is the placebo that many eat, believing it will take away the pain of their spiritual sickness (Second Corinthians 11:14).

If you look around there isn't any shortage of experiencing upper hell, even with belief bias minimizing the pain. Clearly, everyone pays an exorbitant price to live selfishly. Yet how many people witness in believers the undeniable evidence that lower heaven is worth surrendering to God's parenting?

Christians are meant to reveal fruit that is irrefutably the richest blessings this life has to offer. If Christians focused on living selflessly (not on exposing the world's sin that they painfully know all too well), everyone would see Jesus with skin on. Then, the world would see firsthand what they are missing when choosing independence before they are forced to bow their knees and confess, "Jesus is King."

How much eye-catching fruit are Christians producing that proves Christ is who He says He is, and did what He says He did? "That they may be one just as We are one: I in them, and You in Me; that they may be made perfect in one, and that the world may know that You have sent Me, and have loved them as You have loved Me" (John 17:22-23).

23

Heaven's Appetizers

God offers several opportunities for all mankind to sample appetizers of heaven and hell before dying. Appetizers of hell are obvious: Anger, fear, distrust, depression, lust, coveting, and jealousy, etc.

God gives several appetizers to wet our appetite for heaven. First the joy we experience when we obey His leading. And the beauty of nature points to a God Who wants to bless us. The freedom from sin's enslavements. We witness God pouring through His children producing beautiful glimpses of heaven. God's written Word reveals a great deal of God's loving nature, what we can expect in heaven. Etc.

Arguably, God's greatest revelation of Himself relates to mankind's deep desire to experience oneness. And, only His selfless produces unbreakable oneness. We all yearn to be loved and to love. Someone we know who will walk through the fire with us. To have their pain and joy in our hearts, and visa versa. Nothing means more. When choosing selfless or selfish love, we all sample either heaven or hell, leaving no room for the argument of ignorance (Acts 14:16-17, 17:23-30; Romans 2:14-15; Titus 2:11).

Those who make Christ ruler of their lives do not fear death any more than they fear a beautiful sunset. One day ends in a beautiful fashion with the promise of a greater one dawning. They eagerly look forward to finally meeting face to face the person that they have grown to love and trust. Over the course of their lives, they have received His peace, comfort, direction, purpose, love, and forgiveness. Finally, they relish the opportunity to know Christ without any hindrances.

When meeting Jesus face to face it's not, "My name is Charles. I went to the big church on Main Street and I worked on their sound team. If you want to know why You should let me into heaven, I trust in Jesus' cross for forgiveness."

Instead, it's, "My dear Friend, at last we meet!" Then, going down memory lane together, laughing, "We got history! Remember when You closed that door in my face and I almost lost my mind? I yelled at You for a solid month, but then You opened another door that was many times better. That grew my faith for the next time You slammed the door on my nose!" And on and on…

Apostle John states that on Judgement Day God will focus on whether we spent His selfless love on others. If so, we enjoy peace. If not, we fear. Why fear? Not having experienced His selfless love running through us, we have little understanding of His agape love coming from Him to us. *In addition, once meeting Him face to face, we will realize how close or far from His character we truly lived. All our self-driven goodness, given with our selfish ends attached, will smell like rotting flesh. 1 John 2:28, 4:17*

> *Eternal life and eternal death both begin here and now. Heaven and hell are there and then.* A continuation of who we choose to love while breathing, ourselves or Christ.

Heaven will far surpass the greatest realization of oneness that has yet to overcome our hearts while breathing. Perfect oneness with Christ and others for eternity, without Satan or SIN to interfere.

There are some whose marriages are so strong in their love for one another, they can't imagine why God would not continue their marriage to each other in heaven. While a God-honoring marriage represents God's tasty appetizer of heaven's oneness, it is still only a teaser, a tiny nibble of the oneness we will experience in heaven with Christ. *In heaven, the longest and strongest marriage on earth will pale by comparison to the oneness we will enjoy with everyone in our spiritual family (Luke 20:35; Ephesians 1:10; Revelation 19:7).*

Imagine someone who has never visited any ocean being told, "I can't take you to the Pacific Ocean right now, but I can give you a little look. In this glass jar is water I scooped out of the Pacific Ocean. Now, look into this jar and imagine the same water thousands of miles across and thousands of feet deep, teeming with fish of all sizes, colors, and shapes. Imagine huge powerful waves that constantly crash on the shore that you can bodysurf on, and tides that work like clockwork with the moon. Picture when the sun sets, it glistens a billion tiny reflections. It's simply breathtaking."

Would you be satisfied? Would you feel like you don't need to visit the Pacific Ocean anymore (First Corinthians 13:12; Second Corinthians 3:18, 4:6; First John 3:2)?

Meeting Christ face to face will be paramount to going from looking at a glass of the Pacific Ocean to swimming in it.

24

Seeing Hell With God's Eyes

How terrifying will hell be to the person who chooses upper hell now?

Our heavenly Father knows the vast, spiritual difference between heaven and hell. He thought that difference so great that He considered it worth the price of His Son to make a way for mankind not to suffer in hell. In the end, when meeting Jesus face to face, He will make the enormous contrast clear to us and we will fully delight in His love. "Then I shall know just as I also am known" (First Corinthians 13:12).

Will those who chose living self-ruled also feel exuberant when meeting their spiritual father, Satan, face to face and their new home life? Or will they scream in terror? Or, find it a challenge worth undertaking?

Are we swimming our way through hell's cesspool right now? Not until we grasp and enjoy the extreme "width and length and depth and height" of Christ's love in heaven will we grasp that our time on this earth often encountered "going through hell." (Ephesians 3:18).

Remember that Satan, his angels, and his family cover the entire planet like a blanket. Satan is the "prince of the power of the air" here and now that "works in the sons of disobedience" (Ephesians 2:2). Christians are pilgrims, not residents. Perhaps lower hell, the spiritual opposite of upper heaven, is simply where Satan gets full custody of his children without God, God's angels, and God's children around to interfere. Hell happens when Satan, SIN, and his family are left completely to their own devices. Will they cherish the freedom to live self-ruled and happily handle the consequences the same way they do now? They love "dry places." (John 18:36, Luke 11:24, Colossians 1:13)

These questions beg another question. Is the nature of heaven more foreign to mankind than the nature of hell?

How did Jesus and the apostles pray and teach about heaven and hell? Did Jesus ever pray, "Father, open their eyes to how horrific hell is?" Why not, unless we are already neck-deep in what hell offers? Jesus prayed for His Father's kingdom come, indicating this is not it. Jesus prayed fervently for His followers to truly know Him, His Spirit, and His Father. By Christ's prayers, it appears that between the two, heaven is the place we know the least (Matthew 6:10, John 17:20-26).

"Heaven" is mentioned 284 times in the New Testament. The phase, "kingdom of God," is repeated another 75 times. Yet all three different words that are used to describe hell, added together, are mentioned less than thirty times. Which place needs the most explaining?

Neither did the apostle Paul pray, "God, reveal to the world how painful hell is before it is too late." Instead, he prayed for "the eyes of your understanding being enlightened; that you may know what is the hope of His calling, what are the riches of the glory of His inheritance in the saints" (Ephesians 1:18). Paul prayed for everyone to understand the nature of God's love and to turn from what they seemed to know all too well (Acts 26:18).

Why doesn't the Bible do more to try to scare people out of hell?

For someone who deliberately chooses to live with SIN's enslavements now, what added torture about hell itself would deter them? Many have developed a huge appetite for upper hell. To some, lower hell sounds more like a grander challenge than torture. "For everyone practicing evil hates the light and does not come to the light, lest his deeds should be exposed. But he who does the truth comes to the light, that his deeds may be clearly seen, that they have been done in God" (John 3:20-21).

Because there are those who relish the thought of upper hell, you may be thinking that watering down the suffering of hell, making it "air-conditioned," takes away from the beauty of heaven. "If hell is not very hellacious, then heaven loses its heavenliness."

First, does SIN torment us as it torments God? Not close. Not until we grasp the perfection of heaven, we will understand the corruption of this world and hell.

Then, truly ask yourself, "If I removed God completely out of my life now, what do I have left?"

To a believer who has matured in their relationship with their Father, His love is heaven's great attraction and just the thought of His absence sounds horrifying. To His child, life begins with Him and living without Him creates hell. Living with Christ is more essential than breathing. Throughout life, their eyes focus on their endearing HOLY relationship with Jesus, not fearfully running to Him because they see the painful consequences of SIN when looking over their shoulder at the rest of the world.

As to insulting the beauty of heaven, would a Father who loves this world enough to send His Son want the primary reason people choose His presence over Satan's to be based on avoiding torment, not loving Him back?

If God must threaten mankind with a horrific hell as motivation to choose His heaven by default, how insulting is that to the beauty of His Person? God can't compete with Satan so He threatens people into heaven with torment? (Job 1:9)

25

Forgiveness With a Gift

We are repeatedly instructed to forgive one another just as Christ forgave us. Nonetheless, in order to remain self-serving, we have devised several alternative ways to forgive others without truly forgiving them as Jesus forgave us (Matthew 6:12-15; Ephesians 4:32).

Many counselors encourage forgiveness for selfish reasons, stating, "Unforgiveness is the poison I drink hoping someone else dies." To forgive for freedom from anger is self-serving, not God serving. And God doesn't think of us as "dead" in order to not remain angry at us. Or imagine God thinking, "I will get my revenge for your rebellion by loving My life."

Unbiblical forgiveness still leaves scabs with countless triggers that will pull them off. With unhealed wounds, why open one's heart's door to get hurt again? To protect our heart's domain, we learn to trust no one. No one enjoys true freedom inside the walls of self-serving forgiveness.

Others reason it best to let go of an offense because returning evil for evil will only escalate the battle to the next level of evil. Self-serving wisdom states, "Bury the hatchet to minimize your losses. Being hurt is bad enough, so let vengeance go or it will likely get worse." Sadly, unresolved anger turns into depression. "I got done wrong and there is nothing I can do to get even. Life sucks! People are dirtbags." Still far from free.

Then there are those who refuse to forgive regardless of the downside of harboring anger. They read, "To offer forgiveness is to set a prisoner free and then to discover the prisoner was me" and retort, "Me? Prisoner? No way. I want to stay mad! It makes me feel like I am getting even. I love payback, even if it's only in my head." And they reason, "If I forgive all the idiots that violate my rights, soon everyone will walk all over me."

Bondage is worn like a badge and it stinks up their life. When stewing in their anger, they can't savor a delicious meal or appreciate a beautiful sunset. Many become control freaks, constantly manipulating others to protect their frail domains from being intruded upon again.

Forgiving others as God forgives us will cause the "queen in the dungeon" to scream louder than any other act of obedience. Biblical forgiveness is the spiritual acid test, proving who our ruler truly is. *Forgiving others is the nonnegotiable "re-gift" attribute of all the qualities of God because it requires His selfless love in the purest form.* "*If you do not forgive men their trespasses, neither will your Father forgive your trespasses*" *(Matthew 6:15).*

Giving forgiveness is our "proof of purchase" receipt, not patience, kindness, gentleness, or honesty. No attribute of God comes with a higher price tag than forgiveness, revealing a love that only He can give (Matthew 18:21-35).

How does God forgive?

When God forgives us He chooses to completely and immediately remove the offense from our record. No probationary period, no earning forgiveness first, no payback later. There are no conditions that restrict when and how much. No demanding, "Give Me a good reason first." Just our humbly asking and all our debt is gone. God will never rub our nose in our evil at a later date. *When God forgives, we walk to Him and He runs to us. It's the only time God is ever in a hurry (Luke 15:11-31).*

Then, and far better still, after He forgives us, He adds a gift. After God forgives us, He doesn't say, "Now get lost little brat. You annoy Me!" Or, "I can't stand the painful memories I recall every time I see your face. I would rather think of you as little as possible." Instead, He adopts us into His family to live together. Then, He not only embraces us, He gives us an enormous gift (Acts 2:38).

The gift is not heaven. His gift is Himself. He not only forgives us of our sinning, but we can now enjoy the journey together as His HOLY nature overpowers our old SIN nature. The primary purpose of Christ's cross embraces oneness with Him, here and now (Matthew 5:43-48; John 4:10, 17:3; First John 1:9).

If we are to forgive rightly, it must be to please the heart of God, not for a self-serving attempt to rid our hearts of anger. Out of our appreciation for His forgiveness, we re-gift the same forgiveness we received. Our desire is to represent God's love to a hurting world. The freedoms we experience in our forgiving as we are forgiven, are God's added blessings for our obedience (Matthew 18:35; Ephesians 4:32).

Anti-Merited Favor

How does Christ return His kindness for our evil?

Many call Christ's forgiveness His "unmerited favor." Not even close. We start with a far more hostile relationship than "unmerited" insinuates. God forgave us when we lived rebelliously against Him. We acted continuously hostile toward Him to not deserve His forgiveness (Romans 5:5-8, 8:7; James 4:4-6).

To illustrate, unmerited favor is loaning your tools to help a new co-worker do their job better. You owe them nothing, but you want to be nice. Kindness with nothing in return.

Anti-merited favor is loaning your tools to a co-worker even though earlier they maliciously tried to get you fired. They tried to steal your job. Yet you return kindness for evil. That requires God's selfless grace.

We lived in rebellion against God when He chose to forgive us. Anti-merited. To top it off, God removes our offense and then gives a gift, Himself, to enable us not to repeat the offense again. When we return kindness for evil, the world witnesses God's forgiveness firsthand (First John 2:15-16).

Selfishness thrives on the give-and-take of returning kindness for kindness. Selfishness can even flourish when giving kindness for nothing if it makes one feel good about themselves or lessens guilt. Like the charitable feeling of giving a donation to the Salvation Army when going Christmas shopping.

Nevertheless, selfishness finds no air to breathe when considering returning kindness for evil. Forgiving God's way requires selflessness (HOLY) at its purest form, coming from within us.

When a selfish person receives forgiveness for free, they witness how God forgives them. The disturbing question that hangs over their head, "How am I going to make my wrongs right when I meet God? Will I work them off?" is answered.

"I just realized I don't need to. God forgives freely." They see God's supernatural power to forgive through one of His kids and now know that God desires to mend broken relationships for free. Offenses are dismissed without first working them off. No self-inflicted "spanking" required to pay for their bad behavior.

Determining the Gift

The gift a child of God decides to add on to their free forgiveness focuses on a specific end goal-oneness with Christ for the offender. Consider these two basic categories of people that may offend you and how God may direct you differently on what to gift them after forgiving them of their offense.

The first group represents those Jesus talked about in Matthew 5:38-48. "Bless those who curse you."

If the person giving the offense has never understood God's forgiveness and kindness, then the purpose of your added gift focuses on going beyond forgiving as the world forgives by revealing the liberal nature of God's forgiveness. "I know you tried to get me fired, but you can still borrow my tools. I won't hold it against you. I want to help you."

After they have received free forgiveness with an extra gift from you, they now understand they no longer must walk the path alone in their guilt and that God is unreasonably kind. *Not only is God not angry with them, He wants to bless them.* They no longer are trying to accumulate an unknown amount of good works, hoping to appease their demanding Creator. Instead, they realize they can walk in harmony with their heavenly Father who is eager to forgive and bless. God loves to forgive and then give. He wants to give them a life they love (Romans 2:4).

The second group represents those Jesus talked about in Matthew 18:15-17. "If your brother sins against you."

The second group has already received God's grace and goodness. For this group, the purpose of your gift is not to reveal His free forgiveness or great kindness again, but to encourage that person to behave like family. They need to stop the behavior that dishonors who they claim as their Father. *The added gift given constitutes loving correction, which is rarely an easy gift to give.* Forgiveness of the offense is always granted, but the gift given afterwards focuses on growing obedience. Again, oneness with Christ is the goal (Galatians 6:1-5).

For example: If a believer gossips nasty things about you, you might invite them out to lunch to learn how they are doing. You hear their struggles in their life, giving you an opportunity to share how God brought you through similar problems. You direct them in overcoming their anger. After lunch, you pray together in the parking lot for pure hearts.

……………….

What about those who reject the gift? Suppose a neighbor steals your bike and you kindly forgive them and even give them the tire pump, but they reject the opportunity to change and only want to take more. This is when you get alone with God and ask for wisdom. Do you turn the other cheek again or walk away? Should the governmental authorities be brought in to handle the problem? How about receiving wisdom from church leaders? Always go to God and pray with no heart of your own in the matter on how to best draw them into a closer relationship with God (Matthew 7:6; First Peter 2:25).

"Do good to those who hate you" and forgiving with a gift are never forgiving someone then helping them do the wrong thing. To encourage someone to live in disobedience to God remains unloving. We always offer forgiveness, but our added gift must not usurp God's interests in the person. His interest in people must become our interest. If we aim at pleasing others over pleasing God, then we reverse the two greatest commandments and, in doing so, we destroy both (Proverbs 22:3, 27:6; Matthew 5:44; Romans 2:1-5; Second Peter 2:22).

Forgiveness with a Gift

Sometimes those we love live under the bondage to SIN. We think that we are being kind to them by generously forgiving them. We find ourselves afraid of upsetting them with painful discipline, but God is interested in growing a person from selfish to selfless.

Consider a few examples. Parents enabling their adult children to live carelessly in their home while avoiding responsibility. Spouses turning a blind eye to each other's bad habits. Church board members afraid to address the faults of the leadership. *Only sin supports sin* (Galatians 6:1; First Timothy 5:19).

Jesus mercifully healed all those who came to Him, regardless of their obedience, and He taught that His Father is kind to the unthankful and evil (Luke 6:35*). How do we reconcile God's generosity to those who live in disobedience, while not encouraging someone to live in disobedience?* Clearly, there are many scriptures that describe God using discipline to change our hearts and minds (Proverbs 3:12; Hebrews 12:6; Revelation 3:19).

In spite of witnessing God's kindness, our birth nature still screams, "You must stay in charge to get what you want." To shake someone out of their hardhearted state, God often mercifully resorts to using a great deal of pain to get their attention. For this reason, God may have His children give over the hardhearted offender to the painful consequences of their self-serving rebellion against God (First Corinthians 5:5).

Sometimes a believer, thinking themselves loving toward a hurting person, puts a "book in their pants" when God wants to spank them. "I will pay for your DUI attorney." God is not pleased. They are not truly helped and we often feel the sting of someone else's sin.

……………….

Does returning kindness for evil sound unreasonable? Is forgiveness with a gift asking too much of an injured soul? In this world, we are to expect to be treated as Christ was treated. Therefore, we depend on Christ to carry us through the times we need His supernatural grace. How else will the world know we are filled with His Spirit if nothing we do requires another source? "But when you do good and suffer, if you take it patiently, this is commendable before God" (First Peter 2:20).

When struggling to forgive with a gift, remember the ridiculous price God the Father, the Son, and the Holy Spirit choose to pay to reveal their quality of forgiveness. In the sinless Garden of Eden, the only attribute they couldn't reveal was forgiveness. They could show their love, kindness, goodness, gentleness, power, and faithfulness. What did it cost them to add "forgiveness with a gift" to the list? An enormous amount, and still paying. Satan's rebellion, as well as Adam and Eve's fall, were all part of God's purpose to reveal His grace. Jesus is the Lamb slain before the foundation of the world. (First Peter 1:19-20; Revelation 13:8).

Forgiving Oneself

Here is a short but important review on forgiving oneself.

Have you ever heard someone cry in their guilt, "I know God forgives me, but I just can't forgive myself"? Or the advice, "You need to quit beating yourself up and learn to forgive yourself"? Both sound humble. The first sentence is true, but the second is nonsense, though not for the reason most people think.

The Bible never tells us to forgive ourselves. After receiving the forgiveness that Christ offers us based on His cross, what acts of sinning remain to "forgive yourself" for? And where exactly did you think you might get this powerful forgiveness from? Did you do something so nasty that Christ's cross didn't get it covered? Was Christ's cross not quite powerful enough to cover your really embarrassing offenses and you feel you can redeem your pride by doing some very sacrificial work? The insult to Christ is huge (Hebrews 9:22).

In all fairness, the thought to forgive myself is sometimes naively guilt-driven. When a young child lies to their mother, they feel that not until after their mother disciplines them is their offense paid for. And, the discipline fits the offense. A big lie means a really hard spanking.

With that conditioning, when someone says, "Christ forgives me of all my sins," then adds, "but I just can't forgive myself," they are often saying they still feel guilty for certain offenses that require a "really hard spanking" to rid themselves of their guilt.

What we must understand is that every ounce of God's wrath against our rebellion was unleashed on His Son. Jesus did not drop down out of heaven as an adult, live large as a powerful king, then instantly die as He fell on His own sword.

His life was incredibly humble. His death was agonizing and ignoble. As planned before the foundations of the world, He excruciatingly suffered to the greatest degree as physically and spiritually possible. "For the joy that was set before Him endured the cross, despising the shame" (Isaiah 53:1-10, Hebrews 12:2).

Physically, He didn't refuse one lash of the whip when they ripped apart His body. When offered the hyssop on the sponge to relieve the pain, He refused. He bodily endured the cross to His last breath. Jesus took no shortcuts to prove His love.

Spiritually, Jesus was tormented beyond measure. All the shameful, gut-wrenching guilty feelings we experience when hurting someone we love, He took on Himself. The greatest agony to crush Jesus' spirit took place when His Father forsook Him as He placed all our rebellion on Him. "My God, My God, why have You forsaken Me?" Eternal oneness was broken, making us one with Him eternally (Isaiah 53:4-12; Romans 10:3-4; Philippians 2:4-10; Hebrews 10:12; First Peter 3:18; First John 2:1-2).

When we remember a terrible offense that we think needs a "good hard spanking," we must remember that Christ paid physically and spiritually in full to remove that offense. Christ did what we could never do if spanked a million times for one offense. And He did so freely, because He loves us (Romans 5:9, 8:1; First Thessalonians 5:9).

Sometimes, the desire to "forgive myself" remains driven by pride. Only offended pride seeks to forgive itself by doing some make-up work. "That really doesn't represent the real me. I am better than that and I can prove it."

True humility says, "That was me, not beneath me. I made those decisions. In fact, I am capable of far worse. I need forgiveness for all my offenses and I desperately need a new ruler." We're reminded in James 4:6, "God resists the proud, but gives grace to the humble" (see also First Corinthians 13:1-3 and Galatians 3:3).

Only by humbly receiving Christ's forgiveness for free will we freely give His forgiveness to others. If we require a good hard spanking or demand of ourselves some added work to receive forgiveness from Christ for our embarrassing offenses, then we will not have God's free forgiveness in ourselves to give to others. Our guilt and pride necessarily force us to live in bondage between God, others, and ourselves. And, with grave concern, it begs the question if we ever received God's forgiveness to begin with (Matthew 18:21-35).

As stated earlier, Jesus, being the Son of God, is infinite, making His death an endless payment, covering all sins. All the sins of the world throughout all time could never exhaust His limitless forgiveness. Further, being born of a virgin without a SIN nature, His sacrifice was HOLY—the spotless lamb of God.

Just as the Father harbors no anger against His Son, He harbors no anger against us. "As He is, so are we in this world" (First John 4:17). Instead, His heart grieves when we yield to our old SIN nature by sinning. For our sake, He lovingly disciplines us.

God's discipline is never retaliation. When God disciplines our SIN and sinning, He is after our hearts that made those love decisions. God's discipline resembles the mercy a doctor uses when painfully cutting out cancer, not a person wounding an adversary. God's discipline is motivated by love and concern for our overall wellbeing, so He is willing for us to hurt in order to heal.

In the same way, we love the saint who rebels, holding them responsible for all their love decisions, and hate the hindering effects of SIN and sinning on the believer's relationship with God. God cannot bless them as He so deeply desires and they suffer, living in upper hell.

Oneness says, "If God hates SIN and sinning, then so do I." And, "If God loves the person yielding to SIN and sinning, then so do I." And, "How God wants me to forgive with a gift, that is how I want to forgive" (John 1:9, 29, 3:36; First Timothy 2:4-6; Hebrews 2:9; Second Peter 2:1-8; First John 2:2).

Forgive and Forget?

Another common misconception is that we must "forgive and forget." The Bible never asks us to forget.

Often, people think they have not forgiven someone because they have not forgotten the offense. Is it feasible for a woman who gives birth to a child conceived from a rape to forget how her precious ten-year-old child was conceived? Can someone that loses their leg after being hit by a drunk driver forget, even fifty years later, where their leg disappeared to? God forgets our sins, but only in the sense that He will never bring them back to condemn us. God doesn't suffer from memory loss.

If true forgiveness is given, remembering an offense loses its sting more and more. As someone prays for God's heart in the matter and returns kindness for evil as God directs, they will start to develop a supernatural love for the very person they should hate.

In time, remembering the offense will evolve into a confident feeling of being spiritually strong. "I have the spiritual muscle to overcome what others may do to hurt me. I am healable. In fact, I heal stronger. I can love freely and not fear being devastated if I'm hurt. I am free to love because I am free to forgive." With God's forgiveness within us, our hearts are not just healable, but heal stronger and pass His healing on to others.

Kindness for Evil in the Old Testament

Is returning kindness for evil found only in the New Testament, subsequent to Christ's cross, or is it also established in the Old Testament?

Out of jealousy King Saul actively pursued David with his army to murder him. David had an easy opportunity to kill King Saul and take his place as king, yet David refused. Instead of returning evil for evil, David returned kindness for evil. Saul said to David, "You are more righteous than I; for you have rewarded me with good, whereas I have rewarded you with evil" (First Samuel 24:17). David also returned kindness for evil to his son, Absalom (Second Samuel 18:5). No wonder God calls David a man after His own heart (First Kings 11:4).

During the time when Job was being tested by God and Satan, he was harassed at length by three very foolish counselors. After Job remained faithful during his test, he prayed for his accusers to be judged kindly by God for their foolishness. After Job returned kindness for evil, "the Lord gave Job twice as much as he had before" (Job 42:10).

Joseph was sold into slavery by his own brothers. Years later, Joseph becomes a ruler in Egypt and now the brothers are fearfully begging for their lives. "Joseph said to them, 'Do not be afraid, for am I in the place of God? But as for you, you meant evil against me; but God meant it for good, in order to bring it about as it is this day...do not be afraid; I will provide for you and your little ones'" (Genesis 50:19-21).

Do you desire to hit the bullseye of the heart of God? Then offer forgiveness with a gift—kindness for evil. If you do, you will experience God's supernatural power like never before and live in the freedom God meant for you to enjoy.

26

Bypassing Words

The life changing experiences that overpower our emotions will always surpass our largest dictionary for adequate explanation.

The same painful experience felt by different people may cause one to stand paralyzed and numb, another to cry hysterically, some to collapse to their knees, and others to curl into a fetal position and groan intensely. But for all, words could never fully express their anguish.

A joyful experience may cause some people to jump ecstatically, others to cover their tearful faces in disbelief, some may run and shout, and others may melt in relief. But they also share a common thread. No words will ever come within a million miles of adequately explaining what overwhelmed their souls.

Any attempt to fully describe what overcomes us emotionally remains impossible. What about intellectually?

Have you ever looked at someone's face while an astronomer attempts to describe our vast universe? The "bazillion" number of galaxies they believe exist? Or how enormous stars are compared to our puny earth? And how many trillion stars fly around at ridiculous speeds in the universe? Or how many miles per hour the earth spins as it rotates around the sun? They exclaim, "Wow! That's incredible," but really their minds shut down after "bazillion" from overload. Their eyes stare wide open with the "deer in the headlights" look.

If our words fail miserably to communicate our most incredible realities and strongest emotions to each other, then imagine how easily overwhelmed our finite minds become when attempting to understand God's infinite nature (Matthew 16:17; Luke 10:21; Ephesians 3:3-5).

God's written Word, as life-changing as it is, can only feebly attempt to describe His splendid nature and power. God shares His love and greatness page after page, but our elementary words fail miserably to do His person justice.

To bypass our written language barrier, God must step into the infinite part of our being and reveal Himself. The deepest part of us that never dies. Our spirit that lives on to declare, "I am still here," even after a nuclear bomb disintegrates our entire body into vapor.

To illustrate the mind's inability to grasp the power of God's nature, try to mentally comprehend God's immeasurable love by simply reading the following text without His Spirit's assistance. *First, God's love permitted one person to stand as a substitute of another for their offense. Further, He even provided the person that paid for the offender. Not only that, but He actually became that person. And, beyond all possible explanation, God alienated His own Son from Himself to make it happen. And for who?*

For a people who are continually rebellious and ungrateful. He wanted to reveal the incredible depths of His love in the hope of the world loving Him back. Inconceivably, the Creator of the universe willingly placed those, who intentionally rejected His kindness and grieved Him, before Himself, without regret. Until God's Spirit reveals the mind-boggling love behind those words, they hold less power than the words on the menu at your favorite restaurant (Matthew 10:20; First Corinthians 2:11; James 1:5-6; First Peter 1:12).

Combining His written Word with His wordless personal illumination of Himself, we enjoy an appetizer of eternal life, or lower heaven. The following list contains a few examples of the indescribable power imparted within our hearts through God's wordless revelation of Himself.

- God wipes out someone's overwhelming guilt, removes their mountain of shame, and replaces it with His joy.
- Feeling God's strength imparts an unshakable peace that floods the soul, while standing dead-center in a life-threatening storm.
- God's peace overcomes one's heart that all is good, even after praying thousands of prayers and receiving just as many painful "no" answers back.

- God's power provides inexplicable freedom in our souls to give the gift of kindness to someone who we should want dead.
- God's divine wisdom implants a supernatural understanding, without our reading new information or leaving any tracks that He was the messenger.
- God causes His heart's attitudes just to "dawn" on us, leading to freedom from bondage and oneness with Him.
- God holds our souls in perfect peace, looking square at death, but beyond it with the eager expectation of meeting our loving Friend.

Someone may question, "If God reveals Himself best through His Spirit, then why read His written Word? Is reading God's written Word like picking through a trashcan of words to put a meager meal together, when we can experience gourmet dining with God Himself via His Holy Spirit?" No.

The Bible is the only book that comes with the Author, and that Author loves the reader.

The difference is everything. Black ink on white paper comes alive with life-changing power when God speaks His truth past our eyes and alphabet and into our souls. *Mental comprehension alone amounts to a drowning man clutching a pencil in hopes of staying afloat, but Spirit sensitive believers apprehend God's heart as He enlightens our hearts as we read (Romans 8:5-10; Jude 20-21).*

God's written Word constitutes the perfect food necessary for a baby to grow spiritually healthy. Once we're mature, His Word continues to nourish our souls. As poor nourishment will harm a child's development, how much more will a poor Word diet hinder our spiritual development (Second Timothy 3:16-17)?

God's written Word embodies His soulful nourishment for the reader to understand the nature of His heart, receive it, and then walk it out. In obedience, we become the will of God instinctively, realizing His unspeakable power flowing through as we obey. Are we properly nourished by His written Word? If not, we will struggle discerning His heart's nature and wisdom. Our discernment will often fail to determine half-truths. We will live at the mercy of teachers who distort His selfless heart with their selfish interests.

The self-evident fact that anything of true power is necessarily beyond expressing in words clearly tells us we are made far deeper than our finite minds can grasp. Deep calls to deep. We are created to live more profoundly and completely, enjoying a greater reality than our infantile natural view of reality. We possess an infinite side, the part of us that lives eternally, that God supernaturally communicates His powerful truths to (Psalm 42:1-5; First Corinthians 2:10; Second Corinthians 5:2, 4).

If our spiritual lives must survive within the limits our words, how can we witness that God has touched us with His power? *But after receiving His life altering revelations in us, we are in the helpless position of attempting to express*

His true nature in words to someone else. Christianity embraces a supernatural person to person relationship that surpasses words. Why would we expect anything less? (Romans 8:26, 11:33-36; Galatians 4:6)

Final Thoughts

How badly do you want to be free?

Christ's cross provided a way to rid our lives of shame and guilt. If we humble down and leave our shame and guilt at Calvary, He will set us free. But, not simply free from bondage, free to walk in oneness with Him.

Enjoying His freedom requires deciding to obey God's selfless nature over our selfish birth nature. Giving up living for our domains to living to serve His Kingdom. Self-rule for Christ-rule.

Simply because we want the blessings of living free from fear, anger, depression, and aimlessness doesn't mean we are willing to give up our self-rule to no longer live self-serving. To know how to serve Him, we learn how to ask Him questions with no heart of your own in the matter.

As we yield to Christ within us, we flow in His holy nature, follow His specific leading, and impress His heart. On the other side of obedience, we will absolutely love our lives and others will see Jesus with skin on.

The choice we make is the father we choose to love and grow in oneness with, both now and in eternity. The appetizers of upper hell and lower heaven are our indicators which father we serve.

About the Author

After graduating from business college and seminary, Bjorn, and his wife, Cindy, opened and operated a successful restaurant for ten years, located in Southern California.

When hearing God say, "Time to quit feeding people's stomachs and start feeding their souls," they sold the restaurant in 1996 and shortly after opened a large long-term shelter that houses people who are going through a devastating crisis and want to turn their lives over to God.

This book represents twenty-five years of hard-fought wisdom, often received through Bible study and listening prayer, and heavily influenced by Bjorn's favorite authors, Oswald Chambers and C. S. Lewis.

Practically speaking, Bjorn has lived with and counseled thousands of people who have wrestled with physical and sexual abuse, addictions, anger, suicide, demonic oppression, anxiety, etc. His writings seek out the heart of God to tackle spiritual issues while illustrating Biblical truths using everyday illustrations.

Bjorn has been married to Cynthia for over 40 years, every year even better than the last one. They raised three incredible children and enjoy nine grandchildren.

For all of Bjorn's books visit: www.Houseofdecision.com

www.ingramcontent.com/pod-product-compliance
Lightning Source LLC
LaVergne TN
LVHW041541070426
835507LV00011B/857